JOSH

swears by pretzel dust (page 52) as a surefire hangover cure

BOBBY

is working up a scheme to sell Lemon Drops 2.0 (page 174) to the new folks coming into the neighborhood

THE Last O.G. COOKBOOK

BASED ON THE

tbs ORIGINAL
SERIES

INTRODUCTION BY
TRACY MORGAN

Recipes written with
Nicole A. Taylor

Food photography by
Noah Fecks

HOW TO GET **MAD**
CULINARY
SKILLS

THE

Last
O.G.
COOKBOOK

HMH

MELCHER
MEDIA

Library of Congress Control Number: 2018965990
ISBN: 978-0-358-11761-2
ISBN: 978-0-358-11672-1 (ebook)

Produced by Melcher Media, Inc.
Melcher.com

Art direction and interior design by Laura Palese Design, LLC.

Cover design by Renée Bollier

Printed in China
MM 10 9 8 7 6 5 4 3 2 1

CONTENTS

INTRO

SIMPLY PUT, I'M EXCITED ABOUT THIS COOKBOOK BECAUSE I LOVE TO EAT, and I want to share that love with the world. Whether it's the old-school pizza joint in the Bronx that I've gone back to for decades or the peas and rice I whip up on a random Thursday night with my wife—all food is good and you can take that to the bank! I knew from the start that I wanted food—and the ritual of sharing food with your loved ones—to be heavy in *The Last O.G.*

Besides being the flyest show on television, *The Last O.G.* also happens to be a tribute to many of the family and friends I've been lucky enough to have in my life over the years. It's no secret that a lot of what goes on in the show is based on my own real-life history—including some hard knocks I've gone through. As I like to say, I've been through hell and back, but I don't want to come back empty handed. Behind many of the recipes in this book are nods to people from my past and cherished memories, plus some tricks of the trade I've picked up along the way. That's why I'm pleased to introduce *The Last O.G. Cookbook,* Tray Barker's labor of love.

Now, like Tray, I can throw down in the kitchen. I know how to cook a mean six-cheese lasagna, fried flounder, macaroni and cheese (the right way), Cream of Wheat (the right way, too, and yes, there is a wrong way), and so much more. In fact, your head would spin and pop off if you knew all of what ya' boy could do in the culinary department. I'd even go so far as to say that I can cook better than my wife, but I know better than to step on her toes in the kitchen!

Food and cooking are such big themes in my show because they've been big themes in my life.

Starting as a kid, I'd watch my moms head to work at her little store, Betsy Bee's, and take immense pride in the work she did to feed our neighborhood. Then I learned how to cook in funky ways from my Uncle Michael. That's why he's my favorite uncle to this day. Mike had some mad culinary skills. This made him pretty popular with everybody and got him the nickname "Fatty Love." All us kids would be following him around asking for seconds. Then he'd turn the joke around and call us "McGreedy." I liked it when he'd stay over at our house because he'd throw together these midnight snacks and share them with me. He had a special technique, which he dubbed "wild style." This meant he'd throw together in one pot several tasty things that were hanging out in the fridge. It was about hitting on the right combination. I took his lessons to heart. Just last night in fact, I made me a wild-style dinner with rice, corn, sausages, and graham crackers. And it was all good! Then I realized: this is kind of the way that people in prison have to go about things too, cooking wild style with whatever is at hand and being as creative as possible.

Also, you gotta understand growing up in Bed Stuy we had government cheese, also known as welfare cheese. It came in a giant brick. Don't feel sorry for me though because that stuff made the best grilled cheese sandwiches. We made them so thick but you could still cut through them with a butter knife! In fact, a few years back, I was hatching a plan to tell to President Obama: Listen, if you want to slow down crime in America, just get that government cheese program back up and running. Tastes so good and everybody'd be eating it. But then they'd be too constipated to go out and commit crime. How are you going to go out and rob somebody when you gotta sit on the bowl half the day because of all the government cheese you ate?

Well, maybe the government cheese plan isn't so solid. But I will say that, in general, knowing how to cook could help lower crime—better meals, happier people. What's more, it'll help you keep your woman! If you want to be happy in your relationship, both parties need to know how to cook. If you can't cook, it's not gonna work. Mostly because the most important ingredient in any recipe is love. I'll tell you a little story to illustrate this point: One night when I came home, there was mac and cheese on the table. Back then, my girlfriend used to bake it up good. I took one bite, looked up at her, and asked, "This is Kraft?" Then I dropped the fork. "It's over right?" She said, "Yup."

Love is key when it comes to your meals and food builds unbreakable bonds. I've made sure that the cast of *The Last O.G.* gets together for dinners regularly because it's a way to connect. We're not just creating a funny show with funny references and silly situations, we're also creating and replicating the beautiful bonds people can have with one another. And it's important to foster these bonds over meals. You can learn so much from a person just from cooking and sharing a meal with them.

This show is a movement, and it shows black people's lives in a very real way. We're lifting up the community by making them laugh but at the same time bringing awareness to the not-so-funny parts of life like drugs, prison, and re-adjusting to life on the outside. For Tray cooking provides a path toward redemption, a way out of his troubles, a source of pride and ambition. It's also a way for him to reconnect to his family. His methods may be untraditional, but that's a big part of what our show is all about. The family's untraditional,

Tray's life is untraditional, and so are these recipes— which were created as if they came out of Tray's head.

I just hope you take this book and these recipes as a chance to connect with someone in your life. Invite them over for the wildest meal of their life, and watch how your relationship flourishes. While you're cooking, you'll learn about the unsung merits of Spam, Lawry's, and Funyuns. You'll have fun in and out of the kitchen. If Tray can manage to succeed with a prison-themed food truck, you can have a wild-style dinner at least once a week.

Now, get to cooking and thank me later for your enlightened mind and enlarged stomach!

—TRACY MORGAN

CHOPPED CHEESE DIP

Ladies and gentlemen, my name is Tray Barker, and I'll be your chef tonight. First item on the menu: a delicacy I call the Chopped Cheese Dip. If you ain't never had a chopped cheese sandwich, then you been missin' out. Supposedly invented in the Bronx but served up in bodegas all over Brooklyn too, the chopped cheese is like New York's answer to the Philly cheesesteak. At its core is chopped meat (what folks anywhere else might call ground beef) that's sizzled on a flat-top, topped with cheese, then slid into a roll. With this recipe you can turn the chopped cheese into a whole party.

4 long sandwich rolls, cut into
  ½-inch-thick pieces

1 pound American cheese slices

2 tablespoons unsalted butter

1 medium onion, diced

1 bell pepper, diced

1 pound ground beef

1 teaspoon Lawry's Seasoned Salt

1 tablespoon all-purpose flour

1 cup milk

1 pint grape tomatoes

2 cups shredded lettuce

SERVES 4 TO 6

1. Preheat the oven to 350°F. Place the sliced rolls on a baking sheet in a single layer and bake for 7 to 10 minutes, until crisp. Remove from the oven and set aside. Set aside 3 slices of the cheese and cube the remaining slices.

2. In a large frying pan, melt 1 tablespoon of the butter over medium heat. Add the onion and cook for 3 to 4 minutes, until softened. Add the bell pepper and cook for another 2 to 3 minutes. Move the onion and pepper aside in the pan, add the beef to the center of the pan, and turn the heat up to medium-high.

3. Season the beef with the seasoned salt. Press it down with a metal spatula to form a crust and let it cook for 4 to 5 minutes. Chop the meat with the spatula, breaking it up and cooking off the pink parts for 4 to 5 minutes, until thoroughly browned.

4. Melt 2 of the reserved slices of cheese over the beef, letting them touch the bottom of the pan to crisp up, about 2 minutes. Transfer the cheesy beef to a medium bowl and turn the heat down to low.

5. In a large frying pan, melt the remaining 1 tablespoon butter, add the flour, and cook until it bubbles and forms a light roux. Whisk in the milk. Working one handful at a time, add the cheese cubes and whisk until fully melted and incorporated. Mix the beef into the cheese. If using a serving bowl or warming vessel, transfer the dip. Lay the last slice of cheese over the dip to melt.

6. Arrange the tomatoes, lettuce, and roll slices on a platter. Serve alongside the dip so guests can make their own mini sandwiches.

13

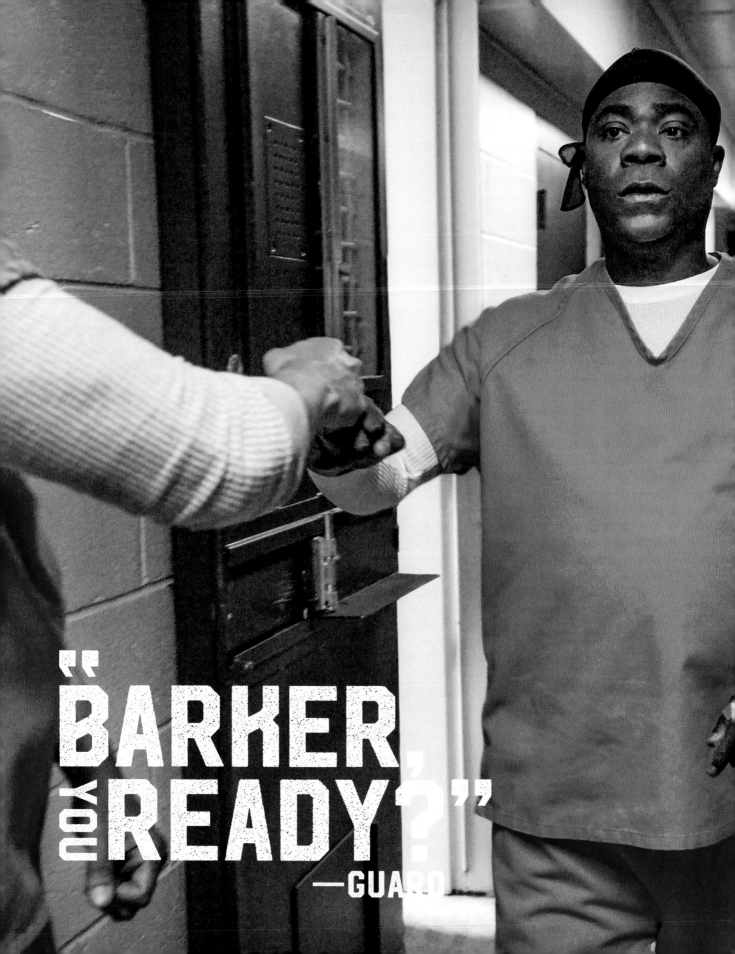

"BARKER, YOU READY?"

—GUARD

"AS READY AS YOUR WIFE IS AFTER A SHOT OF HENNESSY. "

—TRAY

GREEN EYES'S *Fried Pickles*

20 large or 40 small dill
  pickle chips

2 large eggs

½ cup buttermilk

1 cup crushed corn
  chips

½ cup cornmeal

1 teaspoon kosher salt

1 teaspoon paprika

½ teaspoon garlic
  powder

½ teaspoon onion
  powder

¼ cup cornstarch

2 cups vegetable oil

They say everything tastes better fried. I don't necessarily agree with that, but Green Eyes managed to come up with this wonderful recipe for fried pickles. The crunchy exterior is matched by the crunchy pickle on the inside, giving you a surround sound of deliciousness that will not only wake up your neighbors but wake up your taste buds. Trust me.

1. Lightly squeeze the brine out of the pickles into a shallow bowl. Whisk in the eggs and set aside. In a medium bowl, soak the pickle chips in the buttermilk for at least 20 minutes on the counter or up to 4 hours in the refrigerator.

2. In a separate bowl, mix the crushed corn chips, cornmeal, salt, paprika, garlic powder, and onion powder. Place the cornstarch in another bowl. Heat the oil in a large frying pan over medium heat.

3. Drain the pickles and pat dry with paper towels. Dip each pickle into the cornstarch and dust it off. Dredge the pickles in the egg mixture, then coat with the corn chip mixture.

4. Add the pickles to the oil and fry for 2 to 3 minutes on each side, until browned and floating. Drain the pickles on a paper towel–lined dish and serve.

STACKS ON STACKS SHRIMP ROLLS

I don't go to many parties outside of the halfway house, but when I do, I take these tight little cigars of shrimp and beef rolled up and fried. They really make a statement. Like: "I'm bougie, and I'm from Brooklyn." But a word of warning: you won't impress anybody if you make the mistake, as I did once, of covering them in a dish. The condensation will make these soggier than a pair of blue suede Pumas in the rain. That is the only time you do not want to be like Tray. Well, you also don't want to go to prison.

1 pound ground pork

1 cup minced green cabbage

½ cup peeled and minced carrot

2 scallions, minced

2 garlic cloves, minced

2 teaspoons peeled and minced ginger

1 teaspoon soy sauce

¼ teaspoon black pepper

1 (25-oz) package spring roll sheets (12 sheets)

1 pound shrimp, peeled and deveined

1 egg, beaten with a dash of water

4 cups vegetable oil

1 cup sweet and sour sauce, for dipping

1. In a large bowl, mix the pork, cabbage, carrot, scallions, garlic, ginger, soy sauce, and pepper until combined. Do not overmix.

2. Cut the spring roll sheets in half on the diagonal to form triangles. Lay the sheets in front of you with the long side facing the right. Place a shrimp horizontally on the lower corner with the tail sticking out over the edge. Add 2 teaspoons of the meat mixture over the shrimp. Pick up the bottom corner of the sheet and roll it. Stop rolling when you get halfway, then fold the left corner of the sheet over the shrimp. Continue to roll; when you get to 1 inch before the end, brush with egg wash to seal. Repeat with the remaining shrimp rolls.

3. Heat the oil in a large heavy skillet or Dutch oven over medium heat. Add the rolls in batches and fry until golden brown and the shrimp has turned pink, 3 to 4 minutes. Remove the shrimp rolls from the oil and rest them on paper towel–lined plates. Serve hot with the sweet and sour sauce.

WELL SEASONED

Check out these
recipes that let the
LAWRY'S SHINE:

Jaybird's Popcorn (page 20)

Chopped Cheese Dip (page 13)

*Red Striped Fried Shrimp
(page 70)*

It's got paprika, garlic, and onion. But it's so much more than the sum of its parts. LAWRY'S SEASONING SALT in all its fiery orange-hued glory from label to table, is the one item you'll find in the kitchen cabinet of any black person, from Tray Barker to the Obamas. I don't care where you grew up or who raised you, if you pass the paper bag test, the chances are astronomically high that you've ingested Lawry's at least once in your life. I heard even President Richard Nixon loved Lawry's. His favorite snack was cottage cheese (yuck) with Lawry's sprinkled on top (yum). If that's not proof the White House was always begging for a black family to occupy it, then I don't know what is. But, foreal, foreal, Lawry's is that somethin' somethin' that jacks up the flavor profile on any dish from ribs to collard greens to off-brand kettle chips. Also worth keeping in your pantry: Lawry's lighter-side cousin, Lemon Pepper (pictured above on the sides, see Lemon Pepper Drums, page 42). These are the seasonings that keep on giving.

JAYBIRD'S
Popcorn

It's a universal truth: There ain't nothing Lawry's can't improve. Hand me one of Mullins's scraggly toenails, and bet money if I toss some Lawry's on it, you'd think it's an amuse-bouche from one of those Michelin Man restaurants! That's why when Jaybird first placed a bowl of his special popcorn in front of me, I knew it was Lawry's at first sight. Orville Redenbacher can retire, because this gold-dripping bowl of goodness will make you dream of having kernels stuck in your teeth for weeks.

3 tablespoons vegetable oil

½ cup popcorn kernels

¼ cup (½ stick) unsalted butter

1 teaspoon Lawry's Seasoned Salt, plus more to taste

1. Coat the bottom of a large heavy pot with the oil. Place over medium-high heat, add 2 popcorn kernels to the pot, and cover.

2. Once you hear the first kernel pop, add the remaining kernels and put the lid back on. Listen for popping noises. Shake the pot back and forth on the burner for 2 to 3 minutes. It will sound like a lot of popping, then it will slow down. The popcorn is done when you can count to three between pops. Turn off the heat and wait a couple seconds for a few more kernels to finish popping, then transfer the popcorn to a serving bowl.

3. Add the butter to the pot and let it melt from the residual heat. Mix in the seasoned salt and drizzle the butter over the popcorn. Serve warm.

JAMAICA BEEF PATTIE

These Brooklyn streets are getting whiter than ever, but best believe these Brooklyn kitchens are staying black as hell! Y'all's little gentrification can't kill the Jamaican patty culture like you thought it would! Patties—"dem no go nowhere." You can find them all over at a West Indian hotspot, pizzeria, or food truck. But they're even more delectable if you make them at home.

SERVES 4-6

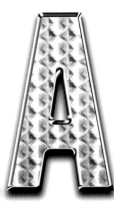
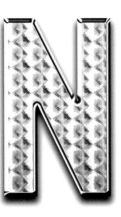

FOR THE PASTRY

2½ cups all-purpose flour, plus more for dusting

1 teaspoon kosher salt

1 teaspoon curry powder

½ teaspoon ground turmeric

¾ cup cold vegetable shortening or lard

½ cup ice water, plus more if needed

FOR THE FILLING

1 tablespoon vegetable oil

½ medium onion, finely chopped

2 garlic cloves, finely chopped

½ habanero chile, seeded and minced

12 ounces ground beef

2 teaspoons fresh thyme leaves

½ teaspoon kosher salt, or to taste

½ teaspoon black pepper

½ teaspoon sugar

½ teaspoon paprika

¼ teaspoon ground allspice

1. To make the pastry: Combine the flour, salt, curry powder, and turmeric in a large bowl. Add the shortening and use your fingertips to rub it into the flour. When the shortening is broken down into small pieces, pour in the ice water and mix to form a sticky dough. If it is too dry, add a tablespoon of water. Knead for 2 minutes until shiny.

2. Form the dough into a disc, dust with flour, and cover with plastic wrap. Chill in the refrigerator for at least 1 hour or up to 1 day.

3. To make the filling: Heat the oil in a large skillet over medium heat. Add the onion, garlic, and habanero, and cook for 4 to 5 minutes, until the vegetables are softened. Add the beef and use a wooden spoon to break up clumps, stirring until browned. Add the thyme, salt, pepper, sugar, paprika, and allspice.

4. Pour in 2 cups of water, bring to a simmer, and cook for 30 minutes, until a thick sauce is formed. Taste and add additional habanero or salt if needed. Let the mixture cool completely.

5. To assemble: Preheat the oven to 375°F.

6. Remove the dough from the refrigerator and cut it in half. Return one half back to the refrigerator. On a heavily floured surface, knead the dough a few times. Roll the dough out to a large ¼-inch-thick rectangle. If the dough is sticky, knead with another tablespoon of flour. Cut out 6-inch circles using an upturned bowl as a guide. Repeat with the second half of the dough and any remaining scraps.

7. To fill the patties, fill a small bowl with water. Add 2 tablespoons of the meat filling on the bottom half of a pastry circle. Brush the edge of the dough with water. Fold the top half over the filling, leaving a large edge. Press down on the edges and crimp closed with a fork dipped in flour.

8. Transfer the patties to an ungreased baking sheet and bake for 25 minutes, or until the tops are firm and golden. Serve hot with a side of hot sauce.

MAKE UP MEAT PLATTER

SERVES 4

One of the nicest things Bobby's ever said to me was, "As a peace offering I brought these cold cuts!" From a broken heart to the flu, there's nothing that a platter of luncheon meats can't cure. It's like a box of candies but for a grown-up. I like the interactive element: You can eat each slice on its own, throw together a sandwich, or fry some slices in a pan with potatoes for hash. If you're feeling creatively inclined, turn the page for ideas on how to make pretty with your meats. Or, you may want to try out Felony's special technique (see opposite).

1 head green leaf lettuce

4 ounces sliced turkey breast

4 ounces sliced roast beef

4 ounces sliced ham

4 ounces sliced mortadella

4 ounces sliced salami

2 tablespoons mustard

2 tablespoons mayonnaise

4 ounces gherkin pickles (optional)

1. Cut off the hard end of the lettuce and separate the leaves. Put down a layer of lettuce on your platter.

2. Unwrap each meat, separate the slices, and drape into piles on top of the lettuce.

3. Put the mustard, mayonnaise, and gherkins, if using, in separate ramekins, then place them in the center of the meat.

SNACK ATTACK

24

FELONY'S LETTUCE CIGAR

1. Layer two slices of meat from the platter onto a lettuce leaf.

2. Roll the lettuce up and seal with a little swipe of mustard and mayonnaise.

► GARNISH LIKE A ◄
GANGSTA

If you go to a fancy-ass culinary school, eventually they'll put you in a class to show you how to adorn your dishes with frilly stuff that diners always throw away—aka *garniture*. I'll never understand why you'd put something on the plate that nobody wants to eat, but I do understand that if you make a plate prettier then people will want to eat more. Don't just think the haute couture restaurants of the world are the only places dressing up dishes. Anybody can bling up their plates at home using some simple techniques and creativity. Raid the snack aisle at your local bodega, and let your imagination run wild. Here are some ideas to get you started:

1
BOLOGNA ROSES

Take circular slices and fold in on themselves until you have a roselike shape, then secure with a toothpick.

2
PEPPERONI ROSES

The fat globules within the meat make these really shine.

3
SPAM STARS

Slice your Spam about ¼ inch thick, fry until browned on both sides, then use a small star-shaped cookie cutter to cut out stars.

4
EASY CHEESE ROSETTES

Pull up right before the shape is done, for the perfect tip.

5
TOMATO HEARTS

Slice grape tomatoes lengthwise into halves then press together to form hearts. Nothing says "I love you" like one of these pressed into a pile of mashed potatoes.

6
VELVEETA CUTOUTS

Take Velveeta slices and use your star-shaped as well as letter-shaped cookie cutters to make shapes you like.

7
FUNYUN CHAIN

Cut some into halves (you could even use your teeth for this job) then lay out the ultimate gold chain around whatever centerpiece anchors your table. Like a baked ham—encircled in a gold Funyuns chain.

MASS INCARCERATION

Tray Barker represents hundreds of thousands of Americans serving extended prison sentences for nonviolent crimes. The policy behind their sentencing dates back to 1982, when President Ronald Reagan initiated America's "War on Drugs," declaring illegal drugs a threat to national security and setting in place new mandatory minimum sentences for drug crimes. Since then, the number of people in America's prisons has increased by 500%.

Among those imprisoned, people of color make up a disproportionate number. African Americans are incarcerated more than five times as often as white people, and though African Americans and Hispanics make up about 32% of the United States population, they comprise more than half of all incarcerated people. Recent research even suggests that when black people and white people commit the same crimes and have the same criminal histories, black people are more likely to be arrested for their crimes and to face harsher punishments.

The effects of mass incarceration reach far beyond just those facing prison time. Eighty billion tax dollars are spent on the prison system each year, and an increasingly expensive corrections industry takes away from other public programs. Over the last thirty years, spending on prisons has increased at triple the rate of spending on public elementary and high school education.

Several organizations are working to undo the policies that lead to mass incarceration and help people who have recently been released from prison get back on their feet.

FOR INFORMATION ON ORGANIZATIONS YOU CAN GET INVOLVED WITH TO HELP, SEE PAGES 216–219.

STAR WITNESS KNISHES

I will never forget when I got sentenced up north, my lawyer brought me a knish and matzoh ball soup. But that knish got me through that weekend. Sitting in a cell surrounded by ten dudes that smell like fifty ain't easy. I remember thinking to myself, this is a Hebrew patty and it saved my sanity.

FOR THE PASTRY

2½ cups all-purpose flour, plus more for dusting

1 teaspoon baking powder

½ teaspoon kosher salt

½ cup vegetable oil

1 large egg

1 teaspoon white vinegar

½ cup water

FOR THE FILLING

1 pound russet potatoes, peeled and cubed

1 tablespoon kosher salt, plus more for seasoning

2 tablespoons unsalted butter

½ cup cream of mushroom soup

½ cup frozen peas, thawed

1 teaspoon black pepper

1 large egg, beaten with a splash of water

FOR THE THYME BUTTER:

2 tablespoons unsalted butter, melted

1½ teaspoons chopped fresh thyme leaves

½ teaspoon kosher salt

1. To make the pastry: In a large bowl whisk together the flour, baking powder, and salt. In another bowl, whisk together the oil, egg, vinegar, and water. Slowly add the wet ingredients to the dry ingredients and mix until a dough forms.

2. On a floured surface, knead the dough for 1 to 2 minutes, until it is smooth. Wrap the dough tightly in plastic wrap and let sit at room temperature for 1 hour or up to overnight in the refrigerator.

3. To make the filling: Place the potatoes in a large pot and cover with water. Add the salt and bring to a boil over high heat. Lower the heat to medium and cook for 10 minutes, until the potatoes are easily pierced with a fork.

4. Drain the potatoes and let cool for 5 minutes, then add the butter and mash until smooth. Add the mushroom soup, peas, and pepper. Mix well, taste, and season with more salt if needed. Let cool completely. To speed up the cooling process, spread the potato onto a baking sheet and refrigerate.

5. To make the thyme butter: In a small bowl, mix the butter, thyme, and salt together and set aside.

6. To assemble and bake: Preheat the oven to 375°F. Divide the dough in half and roll it out into a wide rectangle as thin as possible.

7. Form half of the filling into a log at one end of the dough. Carefully roll the dough over the filling and continue to form a large log. Pat the edges to make sure the filling stays inside. Slice into 2½-inch pieces. Crimp one end closed. Pinch off any excess potato.

8. Place the knishes open-side up on a parchment-lined baking sheet and brush with the egg wash. Bake for 40 to 45 minutes, until the pastries are golden brown. Let rest for 10 minutes; any puffed potato will fall down. Brush the warm knishes with the thyme butter.

SMOKED FISH Fritters

"Ya'll better wrap your mouths around these."

2 (4-ounce) cans boneless, skinless smoked sardines

1 (8.5-ounce) box Jiffy corn muffin mix

¼ teaspoon black pepper

2 large eggs, beaten

1 white onion, finely chopped (about 1 cup)

1 jalapeño chile, seeds removed and minced

1 teaspoon chopped fresh thyme leaves

½ cup buttermilk, plus more as needed

2 cups vegetable oil

Kosher salt

The fanciest food I had growing up was cod fritters, and let me tell you that Red Lobster wishes they could make a fritter like my mom, Rose Barker, could. She'd stink up the whole building, but she'd also have dinner for a week. That's how you make ends meet the Barker way—stretching a fistful of cheap fish into a bucket of fritters. Cook now, and apologize to your neighbors for the nasty fish smell later.

1. Drain the sardines, discard the liquid, and break the fish into chunks. In a large mixing bowl, combine the corn muffin mix and pepper. Fold in the fish, eggs, onion, jalapeño, and thyme. Add the buttermilk and stir until combined. You want a batter that is pourable but not too thin. If the batter seems too thick, add more buttermilk.

2. Heat the oil in a large frying pan over medium heat. Work in batches to avoid crowding the pan. Using an ice cream scoop, carefully drop the batter into the hot oil and cook for 2 minutes, or until the fritters float. Flip and cook for another 2 minutes, or until browned. Remove the fritters from the oil and drain on a wire rack nested in a baking sheet. Repeat with remaining batter. Sprinkle the fritters with salt and serve warm.

PRISON BURRITO

Before becoming famous for my fresh Friday fade from the legendary Siz, I was known mainly for my Prison Burrito. Using only foods I could get from the commissary, I created this savory log of love with chips, snack mixes, and ramen. This here is the worldwide premiere of my secret recipe, so don't mess it up and add anything to this that you can't get for fifty cents!

1 (3-ounce) package instant ramen

1 (9.75-ounce) bag Nacho Cheese Doritos

1 Slim Jim Original Smoked Snack Stick, chopped (optional)

1. Boil 3½ cups water in the microwave or on the stovetop. Set aside to cool slightly.

2. Open the bag of instant ramen and remove the flavor packet. Crush the ramen inside the bag until they are broken down to crumbs. (Or put them in a food processor and pulse to form crumbs, then return them to the bag.) Add the flavoring to the ramen and shake it in the bag. Set aside 1 tablespoon of the flavored noodles and put the rest in a bowl.

3. Open the bag of Doritos and crush them to almost a powder. Take out ½ cup of the crumbs. Add the rest to the bowl with the ramen, then add the Slim Jims, if using.

4. Add 1¾ cups of the crumb mixture back into the Doritos bag, along with 1¾ cups of the microwaved water. Gently squeeze the bag to mix.

5. Roll the bag into a burrito shape and store in a tea towel or oven mitt for 20 to 25 minutes. Remove the burrito from the bag and wrap in a sheet of foil. Garnish with the chip crumbs and noodles for extra crunch.

6. Repeat the process for a second burrito, heating the water up again if needed.

Prison Pad Thai

WHEN I WAS IN PRISON, y'all know I had to be creative. And one of the most high-brow dishes I ever served was my Prison Pad Thai. All you need is some Top Ramen and instead of eating those noodles with the broth, grab you some hot sauce and peanut butter to make instant pad Thai. I've still never had the real deal because this hits the spot every time!

1 package instant RAMEN

+

2 dashes HOT SAUCE

+

⅓ cup chunky PEANUT BUTTER

+

1 CARROT, peeled and grated

1. Microwave 2 cups water in a bowl for 3 minutes. Place the noodles in the water and leave for 3 to 5 minutes, until tender. Use a fork to loosen them up. Reserve a couple spoonfuls of the cooking water and drain the rest.

2. Open the ramen seasoning packet and mix it in a bowl with the peanut butter, hot sauce, and the saved noodle water. Add more water if it does not look like a sauce.

3. Fold in the noodles and half of the carrot, then garnish with the remaining carrot.

1
RAMEN BUNS

No buns for your hamburger? No problem!
Boil some ramen, toss with beaten egg,
then pan-fry in circular shapes. Slap some
ketchup and cheese on them, sandwich with
your meat, and you're good to go.

*If you've got a package of ramen,
you've got the world at your
fingertips. Like a Lego set or a sea
monkey kit, there are all the elements
you need to build something grand.
A bowl of soup? Yeah, sure.
But think bigger.*

2
RAMEN TOSS

Mash these babies up while
still in the package, then sprinkle on top
of a big bowl of lettuce. Open a can
of mandarins and toss some segments in.
Use some of the juice from the can
and canola oil for dressing.

3
ELECTRIC RAMEN

Add Hot Cheeto dust to your piping hot
bowl of ramen soup and let its mojo infuse
the broth, turning it electric orange.
As a snack, Hot Cheetos are like when
Jordan tried and failed at playing baseball,
but, ground up into a fine dust, they become
NBA finals Mike, when he scored 40 points!

4
RAMEN PARTS

Cook just the noodles then toss with peanut
butter and sesame oil, then chill. Boom!
Sesame Noodles. Boil them in some cream
of mushroom soup and you've got Ramen
Stroganoff. Just stir the seasoning into
hot water and you got that fancy-ass bone
broth they sell on the Upper East Side.

5
WAKEUP RAMEN

Amp up your AM by swirling your cooked
noodles around in the pan where you
cooked your bacon, to sop up that flavor.
Serve with your bacon and eggs instead of
toast. Noodles are a 24/7 dish, so why not
start your morning with them.

BROOKLYN

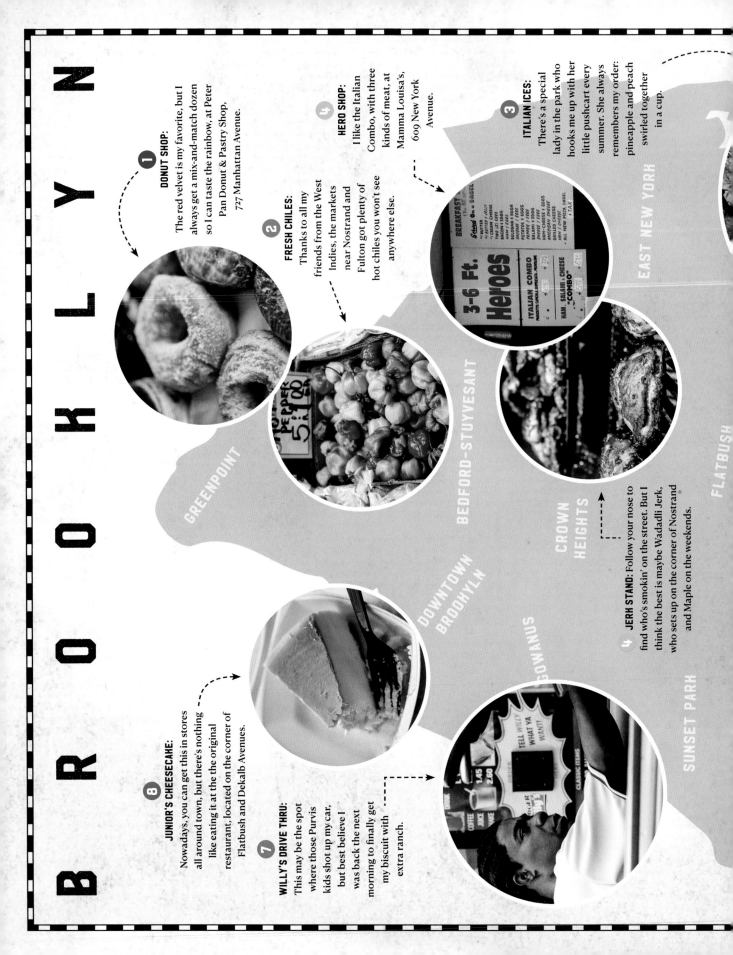

1 DONUT SHOP:
The red velvet is my favorite, but I always get a mix-and-match dozen so I can taste the rainbow, at Peter Pan Donut & Pastry Shop, 727 Manhattan Avenue.

2 FRESH CHILES:
Thanks to all my friends from the West Indies, the markets near Nostrand and Fulton got plenty of hot chiles you won't see anywhere else.

4 HERO SHOP:
I like the Italian Combo, with three kinds of meat, at Mamma Louisa's, 609 New York Avenue.

3 ITALIAN ICES:
There's a special lady in the park who hooks me up with her little pushcart every summer. She always remembers my order: pineapple and peach swirled together in a cup.

4 JERK STAND: Follow your nose to find who's smokin' on the street. But I think the best is maybe Wadadli Jerk, who sets up on the corner of Nostrand and Maple on the weekends.

8 JUNIOR'S CHEESECAKE:
Nowadays, you can get this in stores all around town, but there's nothing like eating it at the the original restaurant, located on the corner of Flatbush and Dekalb Avenues.

7 WILLY'S DRIVE THRU:
This may be the spot where those Purvis kids shot up my car, but best believe I was back the next morning to finally get my biscuit with extra ranch.

GREENPOINT

BEDFORD–STUYVESANT

DOWNTOWN BROOKLYN

CROWN HEIGHTS

GOWANUS

SUNSET PARK

EAST NEW YORK

FLATBUSH

TRAY'S FOOD SAFARI

TRAY'S FAVORITE BROOLYN EATS

Remember the Truth Safari, when Tray takes Shahzad and Amira on a tour of the real Brooklyn, showing them all the special places from his past with Shay? Well, this is the sequel, the Food Safari. Tray's taken a bite out of every corner of the borough, and as an O.G. he makes a perfect guide. You won't find these experiences on Airbnb.

CANARSIE

TACO TRUCK: Check along 5th Avenue between 36th and 60th Streets for trucks and stands. I go for the *lengua*—that means tongue, but don't think about it while eating.

⑤

GREENWOOD CEMETERY:
Also a stop on the Truth Safari, this cemetery has plenty of cozy spots where you can kick back and share a forty with your woman.

⑤

CONEY ISLAND

BAY RIDGE

HALAL CARTS:
You can find these carts all over the city, but some of the best are in Bay Ridge, around the corner of 5th Ave. and 86th Street. Always get the white sauce and the hot sauce. Lamb and chicken together is best.

⑥

NEIGHBORHOOD KEY

① GREENPOINT
② BEDFORD-STUYVESANT
③ EAST NEW YORK
④ CROWN HEIGHTS
⑤ SUNSET PARH
⑥ BAY RIDGE
⑦ GOWANUS
⑧ DOWNTOWN BROOHLYN

Hey, Shay here. There is nothing like a New York City bagel. Every Saturday, Amira and I stop by our local bagel shop and pick out way too many fresh bagels—sesame, poppy, egg, and sometimes even rainbow—for the weekend. But all the true bagel fans know that there's nothing worse than a stale bagel (except maybe an L.A. bagel). Enter: Bagel Chips. These crunchy slices of heaven are the perfect way to give your stale bagels a second chance. Come to think of it, Tray is a lot like bagel chips: old, a little worn, definitely stale. You wouldn't think you would enjoy them, but they grow on you—like a fungus.

1 teaspoon dried garlic

1 teaspoon dried onion

½ teaspoon sesame seeds

½ teaspoon poppy seeds

½ teaspoon kosher salt

2 tablespoons unsalted butter, melted

3 tablespoons olive oil

2 plain bagels, sliced into ¼-inch discs

1. Preheat the oven to 325°F. In a small bowl, combine the garlic, onion, sesame seeds, poppy seeds, and salt. Mix in the butter and oil.

2. Brush both sides of the slices with the butter mixture.

3. Place on a baking sheet and bake for 15 to 20 minutes, until toasted brown and crispy all the way through.

SERVES 2

SHAY'S "YOU'RE MY EVERYTHING" BAGEL CHIPS

Delguadio's
OYSTER HUSTLE

TO ACCOMPANY 1 DOZEN OYSTERS

Delguadio's restaurant is running a racket (besides stealing my Dessert Loaf recipe). They think they can charge forty bucks for a plate of oysters just because they doll it up with some sauce they call "mignonette." I know better. As long as you can get your hands on some quality oysters, you don't even need a sauce. They come with their own sauce—that salty liquor in the shell. Slurp it all down! But if you're easin' into the oyster game, or if you want to impress your lady, you can make a sauce. Here I'm giving out Delguadio's recipe. (Who's zooming who?!) Then I'm giving you a workaround, a bodegalicious option that feels fancy but is a lot cheaper to make.

Fancy Mignonette

½ cup champagne vinegar

2 tablespoons finely chopped shallots

1 tablespoon white pepper

Kosher salt

Bodega Mignonette

½ cup pickle juice

2 tablespoons finely chopped red onion

1 tablespoon coarse black pepper

Kosher salt

1. In a small bowl, combine all ingredients, salting to taste, and keep chilled.

Oyster Varieties

BLUEPOINT
mild, salty, very meaty; great for beginners.

WELLFLEET
briny and sweet.

BEAU SOLEIL
meaty and deep.

MALPEQUE
tender, briny, sweet; may taste like lettuce.

Notes

When you buy oysters, *ensure they are tightly shut. Any that are stuck open are already dead. Keep oysters at the bottom of the fridge in the crisper drawer, store them rounded side down if possible. Keep the oysters on ice at all times once they are out of the refrigerator.*

To shuck the oysters, *you'll need a shucking knife and cut-proof gloves. Locate the hinge of the oyster and wedge the knife in, twist and like a lever, try to lift the top shell up. When you have enough space, sever the oyster meat from the top shell and remove the top shell. Slice the muscle under the oyster so people can slurp it out like a shot. Oysters should smell like a fresh sea breeze. The meat should be opaque and not clear.*

Nestle the oysters in their halfshells within a platter filled with crushed ice, and serve with one of the sauces opposite in a small bowl on the side. Or, serve with Back Garden Hot Sauce (page 148) and lemon wedges.

LEMON PEPPER DRUMS

SERVES 4

It's indisputable that drums are the best part of a bird! (Well, after keel breast, wing tips, and gizzards—see pages 98–99.) Make sure you buy drums (aka drummettes), which are part of the wing. Drums are like Smurf drumsticks, and a lot more fun to eat. (No, I'm not talking about eating Smurfs! What do you think I am, Gargamel?) Also, when you have a fried chicken craving but your pressure is up, these baked chicken joints are your jam.

2 pounds chicken drums

Zest and juice of 2 lemons

1 tablespoon olive oil

1 tablespoon lemon pepper seasoning

1. Preheat the oven to 375°F.

2. In a large bowl, toss the chicken with the lemon juice, oil, and seasoning. Cover and marinate for at least 30 minutes or up to 4 hours in the refrigerator. Remove the chicken from the marinade and place on a baking sheet, reserving the marinade.

3. Bake for 30 to 35 minutes, until the internal temperature is 165°F as measured on a meat thermometer. Switch the oven to broil and drizzle the chicken with all of the leftover marinade. Broil for 2 to 3 minutes on each side, until the edges are crisp.

4. Remove the drums from the sheet. Transfer to a plate, garnish with the lemon zest, and serve while they are still warm.

GUSTAVO'S APPLE & PORK MELT

One thing Gustavo is good for is making a sandwich—even if he does so in his underwear. It may be because there's not as many ingredients to worry about, but the fact remains he's mastered this art! We still don't know if Gustavo knows much beyond sandwiches, but the learning process is slow. Y'all pray for Gustavo.

FOR THE PORK

1 (3- to 4-pound) bone-in pork shoulder

2 tablespoons kosher salt

1 tablespoon black pepper

1½ cups light beer

½ white onion, roughly chopped

4 garlic cloves, sliced

FOR THE MELTS

1 cup (2 sticks) unsalted butter

16 slices white bread

16 slices Cheddar cheese

2 green apples, thinly sliced

1 jar guava jam or 1 can guava paste

1. To make the Pork: Place the pork on a baking sheet and pat dry with paper towels. Coat the pork all over with the salt and pepper.

2. Place the pork in the bowl of a slow cooker. Add the beer, onion, and garlic and cook for 5 hours on high, or 8 hours on low, until the pork comes apart easily with a fork. (If you don't have a slow cooker, braise the pork shoulder in a Dutch oven in a preheated 325°F oven for 3 to 4 hours.)

3. Transfer the pork to a platter and let cool for 15 minutes. Remove the bones and skin—discard or save them for making homemade broth. Pull the pork apart into large chunks with a fork or tongs.

4. To make the melts: Preheat the oven to 200°F.

5. Heat a frying pan over medium-low heat. Working with one sandwich at a time, spread 1 tablespoon butter over one piece of bread and place it in the pan.

6. While the bread is still in the pan, layer on 2 cheese slices, a tongful of pork, 4 apple slices, and a tablespoon or two of guava jam or paste.

7. Butter another piece of bread and place it on the sandwich, butter-side up. When the bottom slice of bread is golden brown, after 2 to 3 minutes, carefully flip the sandwich and brown the other side.

8. Transfer the sandwich to a baking sheet and place in the oven. Repeat to make 8 sandwiches. Slice the sandwiches in half and serve.

ON GETTING BACK ON YOUR FEET:

JAYBIRD: "The mind is our most powerful tool. It's our only real weapon in this white man's world."

MULLINS: "Just what I thought—another dusty-ass street prophet. . . . What you need to be worrying about is getting caught up with some recidivisms."
."

WISDOM FROM THE
HALFWAY HOUSE

There's nothing halfway about the teachable pontifications of Mullins and his halfway house men. Take a bite of their food for thought, and you're sure to be satisfied.

ON THE IMPORTANCE OF SLEEP:
FELONY: "You need your sleep, brother. If you don't sleep, that circadian disruption affects your mind. If you have a sleepy mind, you can't succeed. Sleep and ye shall reap."

ON RESPECTING YOUR ELDERS:
FELONY: "Listen to what the old-heads say. The moe-ron has to touch a stove to learn it's hot. But the genius can see the moe-ron burn himself. . . ."

JAYBIRD: "I see your 'respect the elders,' but I'm gonna go ahead and say 'respect the youth' as well."

ON GLOBAL WARMING:
FELONY: "The warming is caused by all the extra methane in the atmosphere. The culprit? Veganism. Because cows fart methane. But now you got all these cows not getting eaten -- but they still farting. . . . Fish, like feet, get bigger when it's hotter, and they take up more space in the ocean. That pushes up the water, causing hurricanes and shit."

LAST MEAL PIZZA

SERVES 4

When I was 4 months old, I had my first meal and that was pizza, and many years from now, I'll have my last one, and it'll also be pizza. But, I won't waste any of those remaining years kneading dough, so that's why this recipe uses premade dough. You could buy it at the store. But, if you want to keep it hardcore Brooklyn, just walk into your corner pizzeria and ask if they'll sell you some. And remember: Just like me pizza is a true O.G., so don't go playin' around too much or you'll end up with a pizza that tastes like it's from Chicago.

FOR THE HOT HONEY

- 1 cup honey
- 2 to 4 habanero chiles, chopped
- 1 teaspoon red pepper flakes

FOR THE PIZZA

- 2 balls storebought pizza dough (about 12 oz. each)
- 1 cup canned whole peeled tomatoes
- 1 teaspoon kosher salt
- ½ teaspoon red pepper flakes
- Flour, for dusting
- Cornmeal, for dusting
- 1 (8-ounce) ball fresh mozzarella, sliced
- 4 ounces sliced pepperoni
- ½ cup grated Parmesan, plus more for serving
- 4 to 8 sprigs fresh basil, stems removed

1. To make the hot honey: Combine the honey, 2 chiles, and the red pepper flakes in a small saucepan. Place over medium-low heat and bring to a simmer. Turn off the heat and leave to infuse for 1 hour. Taste for spiciness and add more chile if you want more heat.

2. Cool completely and transfer to a jar or bottle.

3. To make the pizza: Evenly divide the dough to make 4 balls and place them in plastic containers or bowls. Let come to room temperature for 1 hour.

4. Preheat the broiler to the highest setting and place a large cast-iron pan on the top rack.

5. Place the tomatoes in a small bowl and lightly crush them with a spoon. Add the salt and red pepper flakes.

6. On a lightly floured surface, knead one of the dough portions for 1 minute.

7. Carefully stretch the dough into a circle, then place it over your clenched fists and continue to stretch, letting the dough fall naturally. When the dough is 1 foot wide, transfer it to an upside-down baking sheet dusted with cornmeal.

8. Dress the pizza with ¼ cup of the tomato sauce, one quarter of the mozzarella cheese, 7 or 8 slices of pepperoni, and 2 tablespoons Parmesan cheese.

9. Carefully remove the hot cast-iron pan from the oven and slide the pizza into it.

10. Broil the pizza for 6 to 8 minutes, rotating it once, until the crust is puffed up, the cheese is bubbling, and the underside is toasted.

11. Remove the pizza from the oven and let stand for 2 minutes. Garnish with a drizzle of hot honey, more Parmesan cheese, and fresh basil leaves, snipped with scissors. Slice and serve while you make the rest of the pizzas.

YOU CAN BUY DOUGH FROM ANY PIZZERIA. JUST ASK!

PRETZEL-
DUSTED
KEBABS

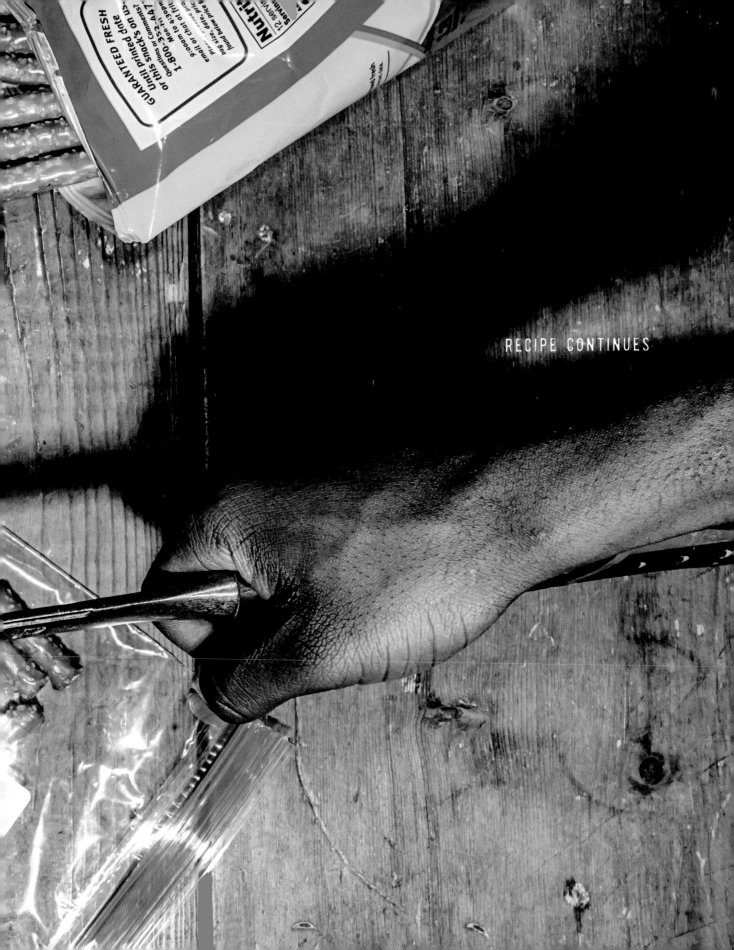

RECIPE CONTINUES

Not that I'd want to, but these lamb kebabs could put every halal food cart in the tri-state area out of business. A bonus benefit: the method here provides the simplest way to work out all that anger you have towards the Man (or towards that fat-ass dude who sleeps in the bunk above yours, Big Country)! There's a hammer involved, but it's used for good, not for busting nobody up. You use it to smash the pretzels for this dish like they're trying to get away. The end result is both cathartic and filling. I bet you ain't that satisfied after therapy!

¼ cup salted pretzels

½ teaspoon garlic powder

2 teaspoons ground cumin

1 teaspoon paprika

1 teaspoon kosher salt

Zest and juice of 1 lemon

1 pound boneless lamb leg, cut into 1-inch cubes

1 bell pepper, cut into 1-inch pieces

1 medium red onion, cut into 1-inch pieces

¼ cup olive oil

1. If using wooden skewers for the kebabs, soak them in water for at least 30 minutes and up to 6 hours. Fire up a grill to medium-high or preheat a cast-iron grill pan in a 400°F oven.

2. Place the pretzels in a zip-top bag and crush with a rolling pin or the handle of a wooden spoon. (Alternatively, place the pretzels in a food processor and pulse to fine crumbs.) Place in a bowl and mix in the garlic powder.

3. In a separate bowl, mix the cumin, paprika, salt, and lemon zest and juice. Add the lamb and marinate for at least 30 minutes on the counter or up to overnight in the refrigerator.

4. Drain the lamb and toss it in the crumbs. Thread the lamb, pepper, and onion tightly on each skewer, alternating ingredients.

5. Place on the grill or a cast-iron grill pan in the oven. Cook for 2 minutes on each side, drizzling with the oil a few times to crisp up the pretzel, for a total of about 8 minutes for medium doneness, or 160°F as measured on a meat thermometer. Let the skewers rest for 2 to 3 minutes before serving.

WHAT THE F*C BROO

K HAPPENED TO KLYN?!

GOWANUS GUMBO

4 slices bacon, cut into ½-inch pieces

8 ounces sausage, cut into ¼-inch pieces

½ cup vegetable oil

2 pounds boneless skin-on chicken thighs, quartered

1 tablespoon kosher salt

1 tablespoon black pepper

1 small yellow onion, chopped

2 ribs celery, chopped, leaves reserved

1 small green bell pepper, chopped

6 garlic cloves, minced

1 cup all-purpose flour

4 cups chicken stock

6 tomatoes, chopped

2 cups chopped collard greens

8 ounces frozen okra, thawed and chopped

1 bay leaf

2 teaspoon chopped fresh thyme leaves

1 teaspoon cayenne pepper

2 teaspoons gumbo filé powder

4 cups cooked white rice, for serving

I grew up a stone's throw away from the Gowanus Canal in Brooklyn. (In fact, we used to throw mean kids' sneakers into that liquid trash heap and watch them sink.) Today, hipsters have taken over the Gowanus (see map, pages 36–37) and act like they're living in Venice or some fancy place like that. I decided to create a recipe for them, a little something to remind them of Brooklyn's real roots. This gumbo may look as murky as the canal, but it's a thousand times more delicious.

1. In a Dutch oven, cook the bacon over medium heat for 4 to 5 minutes, until crispy. Transfer the bacon to a large bowl. Add the sausage to the pot and cook for 3 minutes, then transfer to the bowl.

2. Add the oil to the same pot, get it hot, and add the chicken, salt, and pepper and cook, turning once, for 10 minutes, or until browned. Add to the bowl. Add the onion, celery, bell pepper, and garlic to the pot and cook for 3 to 4 minutes, until softened. Add the vegetables to the bowl.

3. Add the flour to the pot and scrape up the fat and bits at the bottom of the pot to form a roux. Cook the roux for 6 to 8 minutes, until it is dark reddish brown in color. Whisk in the chicken stock and tomatoes and bring to a boil.

4. Add the collard greens, okra, and reserved meat and vegetables to the pot. Stir to combine. Lower the heat to medium-low, add the bay leaf, thyme, and cayenne, cover, and cook for 30 minutes, until the gumbo becomes thick and takes on a dark ruddy brown color.

5. Sprinkle the filé powder and celery leaves over the gumbo and serve with a side of rice.

Love
LIKE
Mullins

HOW TO KEEP
THINGS SPICY IN
THE BEDROOM

It takes a true romantic to have both a love language and a "love luggage," and Mr. Miniard Mullins has both. In order to keep his halfway house tenants from recidivism, Mullins employs a whole program of lifestyle guidance. That program includes instruction on how to live life as a proudly sensual man. Allow Mullins to "Bill Belichick the hell out of you" as your "love guru." His tips may not have worked for Tray, but we'll put a prayer in that they work for you.

IT'S OKAY TO BE FREAKY

But, communicate from the start else you might get scammed. Mullins learned the hard way. "Last time I had a threesome I was the only one that showed up. I went all the way to Connecticut, came back home, and found out they robbed my house."

HAVE A SYSTEM

With all this advice you'll end up with more booty and phone numbers than you can keep track of. So, keep all those digits in a little black book or on an encrypted hard drive. Then back it up online. Soon, like Mullins, you'll have "a whole atmosphere of women" stored "in the clouds."

PACK HEAVY

No, we're not talking about your package (but kudos, if you thought we were). We're talking about what you bring to the event. Mullins doesn't leave home without bringing his Love Luggage—a doctor's bag full of sexual supplies. They have all come in handy on more than one occasion.

Romanticize with roses

Sprinkle a lil' sawdust—
in case it gets juicy

And always wrap it
before you tap it

MULLE
FINGE
LICKE

NS'S
R
RS

They say the way to a man's heart is his stomach and the way to a woman's heart is through her mind. Well, if you cook these finger-licking ribs like I tell you, your woman will be pleading for seconds and thirds—if you know what I'm saying. I'm talking a conjugal visitation. These ribs are the only Afro-deezy-ack you will need. Enjoy and come back for more. I'll be right here waiting with my love kit to share more personal recipes with you.

SERVES 2

2½- to 3-pound slab bone-in baby back pork ribs

¼ cup lightly packed light brown sugar

2 tablespoons chili powder

1 tablespoon kosher salt

1½ teaspoons black pepper

1 cup Mullins' Luv Sauce (recipe follows) or store-bought barbecue sauce

¼ cup bourbon

1. Preheat the oven to 275°F.

2. Cut and peel the membrane from the underside of the rib rack. In a small bowl mix the brown sugar, chili powder, salt, and pepper. Coat both sides of the ribs with the rub. Wrap the rack tightly in foil.

3. Place in the oven on a rimmed baking sheet and bake for 2 hours. Carefully remove the ribs from the oven. Remove the foil, drain the pan drippings into a bowl, and mix them with the sauce and bourbon. Brush the ribs with the sauce, return to the oven, and bake uncovered for another 30 minutes.

4. Switch the oven to broil, brush the ribs with more sauce, and broil for 5 to 8 minutes, until the edges char. Let rest on a cutting board for 5 minutes, then slice and serve with additional barbecue sauce.

THE MAIN LINE

RECIPE CONTINUES

MULLINS'S LUV SAUCE

2 cups ketchup

½ cup honey

⅓ cup white vinegar

¼ cup Worcestershire sauce

2 tablespoons chili powder

1 tablespoon hot sauce

2 teaspoons kosher salt

1 teaspoon black pepper

1. Whisk all the ingredients in a small saucepan over low heat. Raise the heat to medium and cook until it starts to bubble. Continue to cook, stirring, for 10 to 15 minutes, until the sauce turns one shade darker.

2. Let cool completely, then store in a lidded container in the refrigerator.

**MAKES
1 PINT**

Flat Top Fried Rice

Yo, flat tops are dope! No, I'm not talking about the kind Kid 'n Play wore on their heads. *Flat top* is chef lingo for those big-ass griddles they got in all the bodegas and diners. When I got a flat top installed in my food truck, I was as happy as the day I got out of the clink. You see, the flat top is a secret weapon when it comes to browning food. (You can buy a small one made for a stovetop or get a similar effect with a blazing-hot wok.) What most short-order cooks don't know is: flat tops are perfect for making fried rice. I learned this from Benihana. This is my interpretation of their special rice.

4 tablespoons (½ stick) unsalted butter, room temperature

2 garlic cloves, minced

2 tablespoons vegetable oil

2 boneless skinless chicken breasts, cubed

2 teaspoons kosher salt

1 teaspoon black pepper

1 carrot, peeled and diced

2 large eggs, beaten

1 small onion, minced

4 cups cooked brown rice

2 tablespoons soy sauce

4 scallions, chopped

1 tablespoon sesame seeds

1. Heat a large cast-iron pan, flat top griddle, or wok on high heat.

2. In a small bowl, fold the butter with the garlic and set aside. Warm the vegetable oil and sauté the chicken for 1 minute. Using two metal spatulas, cut the chicken up into smaller pieces while it is cooking. Add the salt and pepper.

3. Cook for 6 to 8 minutes. The chicken should be in bite-size pieces and no longer pink on the inside. Transfer the chicken to a mixing bowl.

4. Use a tablespoon of the prepared butter to saute the carrots for 3 to 4 minutes. Transfer the finished carrots to the same bowl as the chicken.

5. Pour the eggs into the pan and let bubble. Swirl the pan to spread them around for 1 minute. Quickly scoot the egg to one side and chop it up using your spatula. Place the cooked egg in the bowl. Add the remaining butter to the pan with the onion. Cook for 1 minute.

6. Add the brown rice to the pan. Stir-fry the rice for 2 minutes, then gradually add the contents of the bowl. Drizzle the soy sauce over the rice and stir-fry for 1 more minute.

7. Transfer the fried rice to a serving bowl or 4 individual rice bowls. Garnish with scallions and sesame seeds.

PAID NFLL OXTAIL

Whether it's your mama or your baby mama, you know somebody loves you when they cook you oxtails and cook them correctly. Make sure to follow the steps precisely, especially when you're burning that sugar. Open a vent to air out your kitchen and make your neighbors jealous of what you're whipping up. Serve this on top of rice or grits (page 75) to sop up all that good gravy.

2 pounds oxtails

Kosher salt and black pepper

2 tablespoons light brown sugar

1 Vidalia onion, chopped

1 bunch scallions, chopped

¼ cup tomato paste

3 tablespoons jerk sauce

3 tablespoons peeled and chopped fresh ginger

2 tablespoons Worcestershire sauce

2 garlic cloves, minced

3 tablespoons cornstarch

1 (15-ounce) can butter beans, rinsed and drained

1. Generously salt and pepper the oxtails and set aside.

2. Melt the brown sugar in a large saucepan over high heat without stirring to melt it, about 5 minutes. Carefully add ¼ cup water to the pot to make a burnt sugar sauce. Add the oxtail and brown it for 3 to 4 minutes on each side. Turn off the heat.

3. In the bowl of a slow cooker, combine the onion, half of the scallions, the tomato paste, jerk sauce, ginger, Worcestershire sauce, and garlic. Add the oxtail and juices to the cooker and top with enough water to submerge the meat. Cover and cook on low for 4 to 6 hours, unitl the meat is tender and falling off the bone.

4. In a small bowl, mix the cornstarch with 2 tablespoons cold water to dissolve. Stir the cornstarch into the stew, add the butter beans, and let it warm through and thicken for 15 minutes.

5. Transfer the oxtails with the cooking juices to a serving bowl and garnish with the remaining scallions.

SERVES 4

Tray,

    I don't even know if I will ever send this
letter, but I needed to write it anyway. I saw on
Oprah that you should write your feelings down on
paper to get 'em out. So here we go. I hate you,
I hate you, I hate you. I told you not to go outside
with Wavy, but no, you didn't listen. Now I'm all
alone. You could've told the police on Wavy, but
you have to live by the code of the streets. What
about me? I actually miss you, and your cooking.
Who gonna make me smothered chicken and green beans?
I've been craving them for weeks now.
    By the way, I'm pregnant, with twins. And
they yours— before you get any ideas. I saw the
sonogram and their heads are big just like yours. I
also know they yours cause I'm craving all your
favorite dishes you used to make. So in summary,
I'm pregnant with twins, I have no job, and my
man is locked up. I hate you!
    I'm going to make it without you. You'll see.
I have to. I just wish I didn't miss you so
much. I hate you.

                                        Love,
                                          Shay

PS— Kelly Clarkson won American Idol. Ha! I told you.
    Justin Guarini can't hold a candle to Kelly. He'll
    never make it in this business. He should do
    cruise ships or commercials.

GLOW-UP GRILLED CHEESE SANDWICH

You may think: ain't nobody need to be told how to make grilled cheese. But stop, collaborate, and listen: The keys to an otherworldly grilled cheese are patience and variety. You need at least three different types of cheese to make it taste better than the diner version, which is actually also delicious, but it won't glow you up like this joint! A hit of pesto and garlic cranks it up too. Take time to let your butter get good and soft, and don't rush the cooking or else your cheese won't fully melt and your bread won't reach that beautiful brown.

½ cup (1 stick) unsalted butter, room temperature

2 garlic cloves, minced

1 teaspoon kosher salt

1 teaspoon black pepper

8 thick slices white bread

4 slices American cheese

4 slices Cheddar cheese

4 tablespoons tomato pesto (or chopped sundried tomatoes in oil)

4 slices provolone

1. Preheat the oven to 250°F. In a small bowl, mix the butter with the garlic, salt, and pepper.

2. Heat a frying pan over medium heat. Spread 1 tablespoon of the butter on a slice of bread and place it butter-side down in the pan.

3. With the bread still in the pan, lay a slice of American cheese and a slice of Cheddar cheese over the bread. Dollop on 1 tablespoon of the pesto, then press a slice of provolone on top to spread out the pesto. Butter another slice of bread and place it butter-side up over the provolone. Fry for 3 to 4 minutes, until golden brown. Flip and fry for another 3 minutes, or until the other side is also golden brown and the cheese is melted.

4. Place the sandwich on a baking sheet and place in the oven. Repeat to make 3 more sandwiches. Remove the sandwiches from the oven, slice in half, and serve.

THE MAIN LINE

RED STRIPED FRIED SHRIMP

Whether it's scrimps, scrimp, scramps, or shrimp to you, these crusty crustaceans deserve our love. Few other foods can accomplish what one single shrimp can. We can eat it boiled, cold, baked, or my personal favorite—fried. Taking a cue from my island brothers, I like to use Red Stripe beer to keep the batter light and crisp. Dipped in a sauce (just about any will do), this sea critter will just scream for joy in your mouth!

1½ pounds large shrimp, peeled with the tails on

1 cup panko breadcrumbs

½ cup cornstarch

2 large eggs, beaten

2 cups Jamaican lager beer

½ teaspoon cayenne pepper

1 teaspoons dried thyme

1 teaspoons black pepper

2 garlic cloves, chopped

4 cups vegetable oil

1 teaspoon Lawry's Seasoned Salt, plus more to taste

2 lemons, cut into wedges

Buffalo sauce (recipe below, optional)

1. Butterfly the shrimp by making a slice down its back without cutting all the way through.

2. Place the panko crumbs in a bowl or shallow dish. Set aside. Place the cornstarch in another bowl or shallow dish. Set aside. Mix the egg and 1 tablespoon water in a another bowl. Set aside.

3. Mix the beer, cayenne pepper, thyme, black pepper, and garlic in a large bowl.

4. Marinate the shrimp in the beer mixture for 30 minutes or up to 2 hours, covered in the refrigerator.

5. Drain the shrimp and pat dry with paper towels. Dredge each shrimp in the cornstarch, then the egg. Let the egg drip off, then coat in panko.

6. Fill a deep frying pan with the vegetable oil and place over medium heat. Fry the shrimp for 3 to 4 minutes until they turn pink and the crumbs are golden brown. Drain the shrimp on paper towel–lined plates.

7. Sprinkle the seasoned salt over the shrimp while they are still warm. Serve with wedges of lemon and buffalo sauce, if you like.

BUFFALO SAUCE

Makes 1¼ cups

½ cup (1 stick) unsalted butter

2/3 cup Frank's RedHot Sauce

1 tablespoon white vinegar

1 teaspoon Worcestershire sauce

½ teaspoon garlic powder

¼ teaspoon cayenne pepper

1. In a saucepan over medium heat, melt the butter then whisk in the remaining ingredients. Keep warm until ready to serve.

2. Refrigerate any remaining sauce in an airtight container for up to 1 week and reheat before serving.

LOADED ONION *Hot Dog*

Now, don't blame me when your breath smells like day-old Funyuns after eating this because it's so worth it and my breath will stink, too! Any food with the word "loaded" in it is sure to knock you on your ass with flavor, and this is no different. Whether you're feening for chips, wieners, or even French onion dip, this jam right here will satisfy all your cravings in one go! I just might suggest passing around some Bubbalicious after you serve these dogs because no one likes a stanky-mouthed bastard.

¼ cup white vinegar

1 tablespoon honey

2 teaspoons kosher salt

¼ teaspoon cayenne pepper

1 red onion, diced

4 ice cubes

1½ teaspoons unsalted butter

1 Vidalia onion, thinly sliced

¼ cup water

8 all-beef hot dogs

8 hot dog buns

½ cup crushed Funyuns

Leaves from 4 sprigs thyme (optional)

1. In a small saucepan combine the vinegar, honey, salt, and cayenne and bring to a boil over medium-high heat, whisking to dissolve the honey. Turn off the heat and add the red onion and ice cubes. Let the red onion pickle for at least 30 minutes before using. (It will keep for up to 2 weeks, covered, in the refrigerator.)

2. Melt the butter in a medium frying pan over high heat. Add the Vidalia onion and cook, stirring, for about 5 minutes, until a brown residue starts to stick to the bottom of the pan. Turn the heat down to low and add the water. Continue to cook, scraping up the brown bits on the bottom of the pan, for another 10 minutes, until the onions are well browned and saucy. If the onions start to burn, add a bit more water and keep stirring. Transfer the caramelized onions to a bowl to cool.

3. To cook the hot dogs on a grill: Grill over gray coals for 7 to 9 minutes and rest them on an upper rack until ready to serve. To cook the hot dogs on the stovetop: Bring a pot of water to a boil, add the hot dogs, and return to a boil. Turn off the heat and let stand for 6 minutes.

4. To assemble: Place the hot dogs in the buns. Top each with 2 tablespoons of the caramelized onion, 1 tablespoon of the pickled red onion, and 1 tablespoon of the crumbled Funyuns, and garnish with the thyme, if using.

If you're in a hurry, just grab a dog on any NYC street corner. Then trick it out with ground-up funyuns.

PARKSIDE

POTPIE

Potpie is one of my favorite dishes because it resembles a dessert but it's actually dinner. You can fool yourself into thinking that you are eating an apple pie when in fact you are eating a full meal complete with vegetables and all that. This is what I call a change-up, and I'm sure you'll love it.

MAKES 8 POTPIES

FOR THE FILLING

1 boneless skinless chicken breast

2 tablespoons butter

½ cup peeled and diced carrots

½ cup diced white onion

½ cup frozen peas

1 bouillon cube, crumbled

2 tablespoons all-purpose flour

½ cup heavy cream

FOR THE PASTRY

¾ cup (1½ sticks) cold unsalted butter, cubed

1⅔ cups all-purpose flour

½ teaspoon kosher salt

¼ cup cold water

4 cups vegetable oil

1. To make the filling: Bring a small pot of water to a boil, add the chicken, reduce the heat to maintain a simmer, and cook for 20 to 25 minutes, until cooked through. Drain, let cool, and cut the chicken into small cubes.

2. Melt the butter in a medium saucepan over medium heat. Add the carrots and onions and cook for 4 to 5 minutes, until softened. Add the peas, chicken, and bouillon cube. Sprinkle the flour over the mixture and cook, stirring, for 2 minutes. Stir in the cream and lower the heat. Continue to cook, stirring, until the sauce is reduced to a thick gravy, 3 to 4 minutes.

3. Transfer the filling to a bowl and chill in the refrigerator for 30 minutes to 1 hour, until it is mostly solid and scoopable, not soupy.

4. To make the pastry: Place the butter, flour, and salt in a large bowl. Using a chilled pastry cutter or your hands, cut the butter into the flour until it forms small crumbs. Slowly add the cold water until it forms a smooth dough. Gather the dough into a disc and wrap it in plastic wrap. Chill the dough for 1 hour.

5. Cut the dough in half and put one half back in the refrigerator. On a lightly floured surface, roll the dough into a large ¼-inch-thick rectangle. Cut the edges clean and cut the dough into 5-inch squares. Gather the scraps and roll out more squares. You should end up with four squares.

6. To assemble and fry: Place a heaping tablespoon of filling into the center of each square. Dab the edges with a little water. Fold the corners together and crimp with a fork to seal. Rest in the refrigerator while you take out the remaining dough and assemble the remaining potpies.

7. Heat the oil in a heavy pan over medium heat. Working in batches to avoid crowding, add the potpies and fry for 4 to 5 minutes on each side, until golden brown. Drain on a paper towel–lined baking sheet. Repeat with remaining batches. Let the potpies rest for 3 minutes before serving.

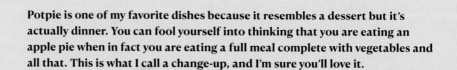

THE DEVIL'S GRITS

SERVES 4

Even though instructions are right on the bag, nine out of ten times, some fool will gum up your grits. That's why you got to take matters into your own hands and make them yourself. You may not be the sprinkling type, but here, you must. Sprinkle and stir. S & S. It's the only way to ensure there are no lumps. Then to turn it into a full-on meal, top your grits with some fried fish and chiles. This dish would even make the devil himself blush.

4 cups vegetable or chicken broth

1 cup grits

3 tablespoons unsalted butter

1 cup shredded white Cheddar cheese

4 teaspoons hot sauce

8 pieces fried fish (page 104)

2 scallions, chopped

8 to 12 pickled jalapeño rings

1. In a medium saucepan, bring the broth to a boil over medium heat. Sprinkle in the grits 1 tablespoon at a time, stirring frequently. Lower the heat to maintain a simmer and continue to cook, stirring, for 20 minutes, until the grits are creamy.

2. Turn the heat down to the lowest setting. Add 1½ tablespoons of the butter and cook for another 10 minutes. Remove from the heat and fold in the cheese.

3. Divide the grits among 4 bowls. Make a well in the center of the grits and add a pat of butter and 1 teaspoon of the hot sauce to each. Place 2 pieces of the fried catfish over the grits. Garnish each with scallions and 2 or 3 pickled jalapeño rings.

Ready for the Repast

They say a person dies twice. *The first time is when they breathe their last breath, and the second is when the trays of macaroni and cheese, collard greens, biscuits and gravy, and the classic baked spaghetti are scraped clean by bereaved family and friends. That's the final, and most delicious death there is—the repast. If you're so unlucky as to lack a black loved one in your life who's died and simultaneously given you the best meal of your life, I'll educate you. A repast (yes, it's "repast"—not "repass," unless you've had too much sweet tea and bourbon at the repast) is essentially a mix between a potluck and a wedding reception.*

Post show, or funeral and burial, the deceased's family members will gather in either someone's home or a church fellowship hall to break bread. You sit around brightly decorated tables and sup the sweet nectar that is the violently red punch mix that includes Kool-Aid, Hawaiian Punch, Seven-Up, and, near the end of the affair, alcohol. But the main event of course is a seemingly endless spread of covered dishes that have been lovingly prepared by a variety of hands. You'll line up among the casseroles and be given the tiniest portion of each by an older woman who may or may not be related to the dearly departed.

How to know when the repast is wrapping up? Folks will start (completely without shame) making up their own to-go plates, covered by either a paper towel or a reused piece of foil and made soggy from the weight of food seasoned with copious amounts of butter and Lawry's. As the sterno cans flicker out beneath the buffet, a deep drowsiness will set in, along with the slight tinge of guilt you have for eating so good after your play-mama died. This, ladies and gentleman, is the repast.

Shay's Repast Spaghetti

Serves 4

The best food is served after someone has died. Why? Because you don't want to be embarrassed in front of the family. Every cousin, aunt, and uncle is there, and they will turn their grief into ridicule if the food ain't right. Shay can't burn like me, but she turns it up a notch for a repast. That's why I was looking forward to her spaghetti at her mama's repast. Now you can too.

¼ cup kosher salt

8 ounces spaghetti

1 pound ground beef

1 pound spicy Italian sausage, casings removed

2 garlic cloves, minced

1 tablespoon red pepper flakes

1 (26-ounce) jar marinara sauce

1 (8-ounce) bag Italian blend shredded cheese

1 ball fresh mozzarella cheese, sliced

1. Preheat the oven to 400°F.

2. Bring a pot of water to a boil over high heat. Add the salt and spaghetti and cook for 10 minutes, or until al dente. Drain, reserving 1 cup of the pasta water. Transfer the spaghetti to a bowl of cold water.

3. Break the beef and sausage up into large chunks. Add them to a Dutch oven or large pot and cook over medium heat for 4 to 5 minutes. Add the garlic and red pepper flakes and cook for 2 to 3 minutes, until the meat is browned on all sides. Add the marinara sauce and the reserved pasta water. Bring to a simmer, partially cover, and simmer for 20 minutes, or until the sauce turns a shade darker.

4. Drain the spaghetti and add it to the sauce, then fold in the shredded cheese and transfer the mixture to a large oblong baking dish (approximately 9 x 13 inches). Top with the mozzarella cheese slices and bake 15 minutes, or until the cheese is bubbling. Let stand for 5 minutes before serving.

"SHAY WASN'T NO ABSENTEE.

SHAY WAS AN ESCAPEE."

—TRAY

Shahzad's Sushi Wrap

When my dad asked me to contribute a recipe to the "cookbook" he was writing, I was dubious. The only book I remember seeing him write in was his numbers book for gambling. Turns out he put recipes down in there too. Anyway, I'm never one to back down from an (easy) challenge. Thusly, I created these sushi wraps that don't require an oven and are inspired by my favorite sushi restaurant, Nobu. I've offered no substitutions, as you should always follow directions to the letter. Please enjoy.

8 large collard green leaves, thick stems removed

2 scallions, trimmed

1 pound skinless fresh salmon fillet

1 tablespoon soy sauce, plus more for dipping

¼ cup sesame seeds

1 tablespoon vegetable oil

1 cup cooked rice, kept warm

2 sheets nori seaweed, each cut into 4 squares

1 carrot, peeled and julienned

2 tablespoons pickled ginger

1. Bring a pot of water to a boil. Add the collard greens and blanch for 1 minute, then remove them from the water and place on paper towels in a single layer to drain. Slice the scallions in half where the white and green meet. Slice again down the length of each piece to make strings. Place in a glass of cold water and set aside.

2. Cut the salmon into 4 uniform logs, if possible. Place in a medium bowl, toss with the soy sauce, and leave to marinate for at least 10 minutes or up to 1 hour, turning it a few times to get at all sides. Place the sesame seeds on a large plate. Drain the salmon pieces and roll in the sesame seeds.

3. Heat a large frying pan over high heat. Add the oil and salmon and sear for 10 seconds on each side. Place the salmon on a plate lined with paper towels, then slice each piece in half lengthwise to make 8 strips.

4. To assemble: Place a collard leaf on a cutting board with the stem side facing up. Spread 2 tablespoons of the rice onto the bottom of the leaf, near the stem end. Layer a nori square over the rice. Place one piece of fish on top of the rice and add a small amount of carrot, scallion, and pickled ginger. Pick up the bottom (stem) end of the leaf and fold it over the filling.

5. Fold in the sides and roll towards the top of the leaf, forming a log. Set aside seam-side down while you assemble the remaining sushi wraps. Cut in half on the diagonal and serve with soy sauce.

CLYDE'S BACKSTABBING RIBEYE

My cousin Clyde, God sort of rest his soul, was one backstabbing mofo, but that dude could cook! If he weren't the one who set me up for fifteen years in the pin, I'd have opened up a restaurant with him decades ago. This fool, as sly and bad as he wanted to be, could stab a ribeye steak in the back almost as good as he did mine. Needless to say, you're gonna need a very sharp knife.

SERVES 1

- 1 pound rib eye steak
- 2 garlic cloves, thinly sliced
- ½ jalapeño chile, cut into rings
- 2 teaspoons kosher salt
- 1 teaspoon black pepper
- 1 tablespoon vegetable oil

1. Preheat the oven to 400°F. Place a grill pan or large cast-iron pan in the oven as it heats up.

2. Using a sharp paring knife, make ½-inch slits across one side of the steak. Stuff the slits alternating with the garlic and jalapeño. Season both sides of the steak with the salt and pepper.

3. Add the oil to the hot pan and place the steak, cut side down, in the pan. Let it sear on the stovetop over medium-high heat for 2 minutes.

4. Flip the steak and return the pan to the oven. Roast 3 minutes for medium rare (135°F), 4 minutes for medium, or 6 minutes for well done. Remove from the oven, tent with foil, and leave to rest 2 minutes. Slice the steak and pour the pan drippings over it.

"AIN'T NO
HONOR
AMONGST THIEVES."
—CLYDE

PAROLE BOARD BACON BURGER

MAKES 2

FOR THE SPECIAL SAUCE

½ cup mayonnaise

2 teaspoons dill pickle relish

2 teaspoons sugar

2 teaspoons ketchup

1 teaspoon onion powder

1 teaspoon white vinegar

½ teaspoon celery seed

½ teaspoon chili powder

½ teaspoon paprika

¼ teaspoon kosher salt

FOR THE BURGERS

4 slices thick-cut bacon, cut in half

1 pound ground beef

2 teaspoons kosher salt

½ teaspoon black pepper

½ teaspoon garlic powder

2 tablespoons unsalted butter

2 slices American cheese (optional)

2 burger buns

½ red onion, sliced into rings

2 green lettuce leaves

½ large tomato, sliced

6 pickle chips

In prison, I knew some guys who'd been in more than ten, twenty years without a parole hearing. And if you do get one, chances are the board will deny you, no matter how much you been studying and behaving right. Meanwhile, there ain't any rules as to how they should behave—they can rubber-stamp you into oblivion just 'cause of the way you look. When I actually got my day in front of the board, they asked me what would I do for work on the outside. I told 'em how I wanted to start a food truck and how I'd cook up the best burger in the world. Well, I can tell you, that recipe must have opened doors in their minds, and it will in yours once you make this.

1. Whisk together all of the sauce ingredients in a small bowl and set aside.

2. Cook the bacon in the oven or stovetop. To cook the bacon in the oven: Preheat the oven to 400°F. Lay the bacon in a single layer on a rimmed baking sheet and bake for 10 to 15 minutes, until crisp. To cook the bacon on the stovetop: Cook for 3 to 4 minutes on each side, until crisp. Transfer the bacon to a paper towel–lined plate to drain.

3. Crumble the ground beef into a large bowl. Sprinkle the salt, pepper, and garlic powder over the meat. Gently toss the meat with the seasoning, being careful not to knead. Form the meat into two half-pound balls.

4. Heat a grill pan or cast-iron frying pan over high heat. Melt 1 tablespoon butter in the pan and place a meat ball directly over it. Using a spatula, smash the burger down to 1-inch thickness. Cook for 4 minutes, then flip and press down lightly with the spatula. Cook for 3 minutes then, if using cheese, add a slice over the burger, tent with foil, and leave until it melts. Repeat with the remaining burger.

5. To assemble, layer the bottom buns with special sauce, a patty, bacon, onion rings, a lettuce leaf, tomato slices, and pickle chips. Complete the burgers with the top bun.

PARADE DAY JERK CHICKEN

3 to 4 pounds chicken parts
¼ cup dry jerk seasoning
¼ cup jerk sauce
1 tablespoon olive oil
1 tablespoon soy sauce
Zest and juice of 1 lime

SERVES 4

Put the chicken in a large container and rub it with the dry jerk seasoning. Cover and let rest in the refrigerator for 1 hour.

Toss the chicken with the jerk sauce, oil, soy sauce, and lime zest and juice. Cover and marinate in the refrigerator for 24 hours.

Preheat the oven to 400°F. Place the chicken on an ungreased rimmed baking sheet and roast for 30 to 35 minutes, until it reaches an internal temperature of 180°F.

There's always some kind of parade happening in New York City, but the one I look forward to most is the Caribbean Day Parade, which is a venerable Brooklyn celebration. The calypso, soca and reggae music gets to thumping as the floats drift down Eastern Parkway. Perched on the floats are ladies decked out in the most flamboyant and skimpiest carnival–style costumes—all in the name of tradition. I love that tradition! But probably my favorite part is the jerk stands that set up along the sidewalk. They spread out marinated chicken inside these special oil-drum grills, which send up plumes of smoke that'll tickle your nose with the lure of sweet spices. Ah, but the parade happens only once a year, and I had to figure out a way to bring that Caribbean vibe around for the other 364 days. That's where this chicken comes in.

SNITCHES GET CEVICHES

8 ounces lump crab meat

2 shallots, chopped

Zest of 1 lime, plus juice of 3 limes (about ⅓ cup)

½ teaspoon kosher salt

1 jalapeño chile, seeded and diced (optional)

1 large cucumber, peeled, seeded, and diced

½ cup grape tomatoes, quartered lengthwise

1 cup fresh cilantro leaves

4 hot dog buns, ¼ inch of each end trimmed

1 lime, cut into wedges

As I continue to reform myself of my prison ways, as Mullins would put it, I'm trying to scrap violence from my payback repertoire and replace it with good deeds. Killin' 'em with kindess, you know? I could track down all the guys who ratted me out and knock 'em around. But that's not who I am today. That's why I inaugurated my food truck menu with this special sandwich. Instead of getting stitches, those snitches are gonna get ceviches.

1. In a small bowl, carefully fold the crab with the shallots, lime zest, lime juice, salt, and jalapeño, if using. Cover and marinate for at least 1 hour or up to 8 hours.

2. Carefully fold the cucumber and tomatoes into the crab.

3. Divide the cilantro among the buns, then place an equal amount of the crab mixture into each bun. Serve immediately with lime wedges.

I use a lot of citrus juice here, taking a cue from the way the halal street vendors do it.

COUSIN BOBBY'S
Guide to
ONLINE DATING

STEP 1
THAT 🔥 PHOTO

For your photos, you want a selection that highlights your best assets. In Tray's case, he has great eyes (for a dude), so we'll want some close up, smizing photos to really bring out his baby browns. And, if you're like Tray, middle-aged, but with a youthful spirit, don't be afraid to fudge some of the details in the image.

STEP 2
PROPS FOR PROPS

Look around for some props and get creative in your photos. The wilder the image, the better. Make it memorable. Add some wine bottles to let your future date know you're fun but won't get blackout drunk on your first date. Perhaps, borrow someone's child to show your sensitive and caring side.

STEP 3
BIO BUSINESS

Your bio should be short! Man, nobody wants to read your life's history, especially if you're ugly! With the bio, like you did with your photos, concisely tell the reader why you're a catch. Can you cook? You got them good massage hands? You got cable? That'll hook 'em!

MAKE SURE YOUR PROFILE PIC IS DOPE!

Tray, 35
Executive Chef, Brooklyn, NY

PRESENT THE PERSON YOU WANT TO BE— NOT THE PERSON YOU ARE!

BOBBY'S

DATE NIGHT PLAYLIST
LOVE EDITION

1. Since U Been Gone, Kelly Clarkson *
2. Someone Like You, Adele
3. In the Arms of an Angel, Sarah McLachlan **
4. Fast Car, Tracy Chapman
5. If It Isn't Love, New Edition
6. Tell Me You Love Me, Demi Lovato
7. Shake it Off, Taylor Swift
8. Pretty Hurts, Beyoncé
9. Formation, Beyoncé***
10. In My Feelings, Drake
11. God Is a Woman, Ariana Grande

* In addition to playing this while running over an old white man, Bobby also played this classic to Tray on the first evening he was home from prison.

** This is the first piece of music that ever made Bobby cry.

*** "I may be single, but somewhere my future wife is listening to this." –Bobby

PORK & BEANS CASSEROLE

Pork and beans is always gonna be good. I've even eaten it cold straight out of the can, no shame. But what if I told you that there was a way to make it even better? That's right, up your pork and beans game by making this casserole from scratch. After tasting this slow-braised melt-in-your mouth pork belly, you won't ever go back to the canned stuff.

FOR THE PORK

8 ounces pork belly

2 teaspoons kosher salt

2 teaspoons brown sugar

1 teaspoon black pepper

FOR THE CASSEROLE

1 large white onion, diced

1 green bell pepper, diced

2 garlic cloves, minced

4 cups cooked navy beans, drained

2 cups barbecue sauce

1 cup chicken stock

1 tablespoon brown sugar

1. To make the pork: Slice the pork belly into ¼-inch slabs.

2. In a medium bowl, toss the pork with the salt, brown sugar, and pepper. Store in a plastic container or zipper bag nested in a baking sheet. Marinate in the refrigerator for at least 4 hours or up to 1 day.

3. Drain the pork on a wire rack nested in a baking sheet in the refrigerator for 1 hour.

4. To make the casserole: Preheat the oven to 375°F.

5. Heat a large skillet over medium heat, add the pork, and dry-fry for 8 to 10 minutes to brown the outsides. Add the onion, pepper, and garlic and cook for 2 to 3 minutes, until softened.

6. Combine the beans, barbecue sauce, stock, vegetables, and pork in a large oblong baking dish (approximately 9 x 13 inches). Sprinkle the brown sugar over the beans. Bake for 40 to 45 minutes, until the sauce is bubbling and thick. Remove from the oven and let cool for 10 to 15 minutes before serving.

KINGS COUNTY Fried Chicken

I'll admit, I got into a little financial trouble when I first got out. But, don't blame me, blame every single chicken joint in Brooklyn. Finally, I realized that instead of buying the stumpy rejects of chicken that I was being served at a marked-up price, I would start cooking my own. And, behold, they're grand. Even Josh, that healthy SOB, goes in heavy with my chicken. Colonel Sanders will salute you if you follow my recipe.

1 (3- to 4-pound) fryer chicken, cut into parts

2 tablespoons plus 2 teaspoons kosher salt

2 teaspoons black pepper

1 teaspoon ground allspice

1 cup buttermilk

1½ cups all-purpose flour

1 cup cornstarch

2 teaspoons red pepper flakes

1 tablespoon chopped fresh thyme leaves

1 teaspoon garlic powder

1 teaspoon onion powder

4 cups vegetable oil or lard

1. Pat the chicken dry with paper towels. Season with 2 tablespoons salt, 1 teaspoon pepper, and the allspice. Place in a bowl, cover, and refrigerate for 30 minutes.

2. Add the buttermilk to the chicken, cover, and marinate for at least 30 minutes or up to 4 hours.

3. In a shallow dish or small bowl, combine the flour, cornstarch, red pepper flakes, thyme, garlic powder, onion powder, and remaining salt and pepper. Drain the chicken, dredge each piece in the flour mixture, and place on a baking sheet in a single layer.

4. Heat the oil in a large frying pan over medium heat to 350°F. Add the legs, thighs, and breasts and fry for 20 minutes, turning every 5 minutes.

5. Add the wings to the pan and cook for about 15 minutes, turning every 5 minutes. Cook until all the pieces are golden brown and have an internal temperature of 165°F. Rest the chicken for approximately 15 minutes on a cooling rack nested in a baking sheet.

SERVES 4

THE MAIN LINE

95

TO DIE DREAMIN CHICKEN AND WAFFLES

RECIPE CONTINUES

Never in my wildest dreams of chicken and waffles—and I've had many, thank you very much—did I ever anticipate coming up with something so delicious as this jam! Actually it involves marmalade, not jam, and a tangy buttermilk batter for the waffles. My point of inspiration here: a special Dominican shake they serve at this Castillo restaurant in Brooklyn. It's called *morir soñando* ("to die dreaming") and it combines milk with orange juice. May sound crazy, but trust me, it's delicious.

2 cups all-purpose flour

2 tablespoons sugar

2 teaspoons baking powder

1 teaspoon baking soda

½ teaspoon kosher salt

2 cups buttermilk

½ cup (1 stick) unsalted butter, melted and cooled

2 large eggs

Nonstick cooking spray

½ cup orange marmalade

1 tablespoon hot water

3 to 4 pounds Kings County Fried Chicken (page 95)

¼ cup powdered sugar

1. Preheat the oven to 250°F. Set a rack on a baking sheet and place it in the oven as it preheats.

2. In a bowl, whisk together the flour, sugar, baking powder, baking soda, and salt. In a another bowl, whisk together the buttermilk, butter, and eggs. Add the flour mixture to the liquid mixture and stir until batter is just combined. It's okay to have lumps.

3. Heat a waffle iron according to the manufacturer's instructions and coat with cooking spray. Pour some batter onto the iron, leaving a ½-inch border on all sides. Close the iron and cook 5 to 8 minutes, until waffles are golden brown and crisp.

4. Transfer the finished waffles to the rack in the oven to keep warm while you make more waffles with the remaining batter.

5. In a small bowl, whisk the marmalade with the hot water to make a sauce.

6. To assemble: Stack 2 waffles and a piece of chicken on each plate. Drizzle the marmalade over the chicken and sift powdered sugar over the whole plate.

WING TIP

LET ME SHOW YOU SOME OF MY FAVORITE PARTS

GIZZARDS

KEEL BREAST
↓

"GIMME A WING, A KEEL
BREAST, AND A BISCUIT . . .
YO, YOU GOT MY KEEL
BREAST IN HERE?"—TRAY

SHAY'S SIX CHEESE LASAGNA

If you have to make up with your man and you don't know how to say I'm sorry, all you got to do is make my lasagna. The apology is in the (six) cheeses. Make sure you go hard with the cottage cheese. If you do it right, he will apologize to you.

1¾ cups cottage cheese

1 large egg, beaten

1 cup shredded white Cheddar cheese

½ cup grated Parmesan cheese

3 cups marinara sauce

12 sheets no-boil lasagna noodles

4 slices American cheese

4 slices provolone cheese

1 ball fresh mozzarella cheese, sliced

1. Preheat the oven to 400°F.

2. Place the cottage cheese in a strainer nested in a bowl and drain excess whey for 10 to 15 minutes.

3. In a small bowl, mix the egg and strained cottage cheese. In a separate bowl, mix together the Cheddar and Parmesan cheeses.

4. Ladle ½ cup marinara sauce into a large casserole dish (approximately 9 x 13 inches) and arrange 3 sheets of lasagna across the sauce.

5. Spread half of the cottage cheese over the lasagna and sprinkle a handful of the Cheddar mixture over the cottage cheese.

6. Ladle another ½ cup of sauce over the cheese. Add 3 more sheets of pasta, followed by the American and provolone cheese. Ladle another ½ cup of sauce on top. Repeat with another layer of pasta, cottage cheese, and the remaining Cheddar mixture.

7. Place the final layer of 3 sheets of pasta on top. Pour the rest of the sauce over the last layer of pasta and scatter the slices of mozzarella cheese over it.

8. Cover the pan with foil and bake for 30 minutes. Remove the foil and bake for an additional 5 to 10 minutes, until the cheese is bubbling. Let the lasagna stand for 5 minutes before cutting.

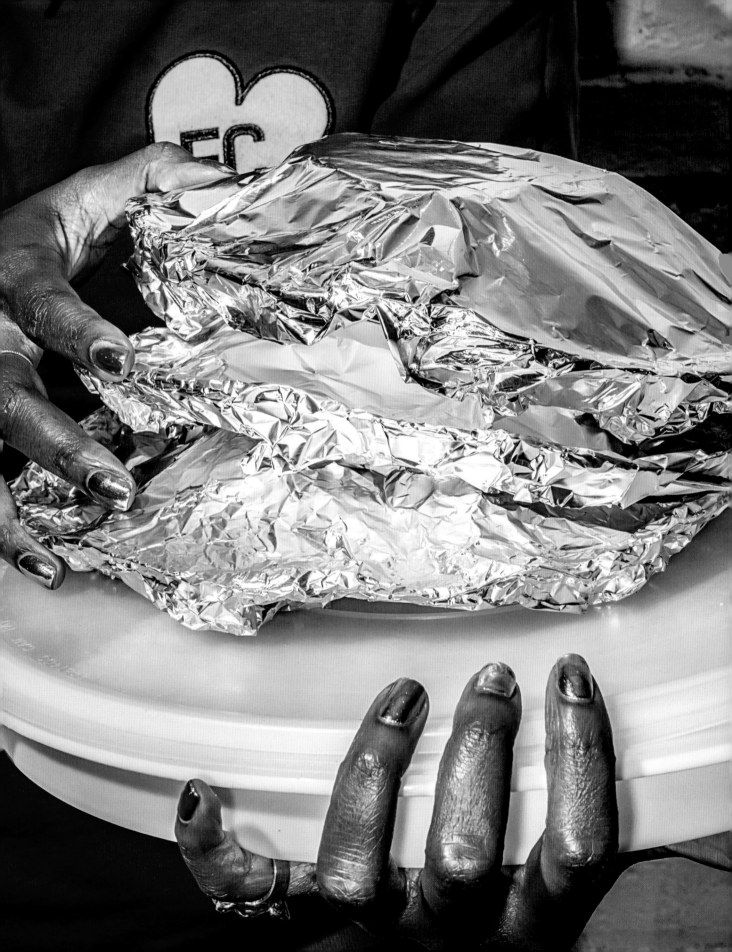

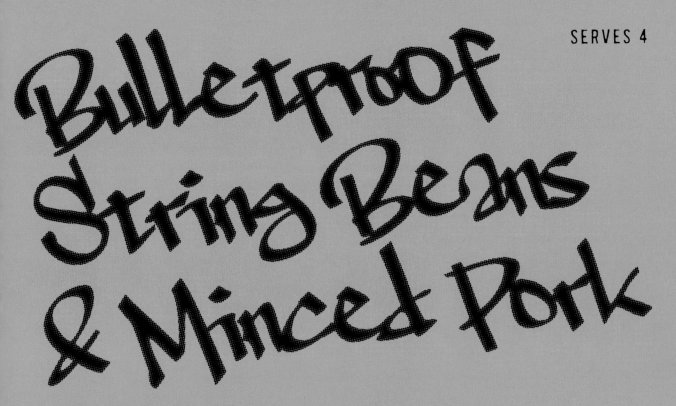

Bulletproof String Beans & Minced Pork

SERVES 4

In case anyone ever accuses you of eating unbalanced meals, point them in the direction of this dish. All it's missing is a carb, but Jaybird says that we should be cutting down on those anyway. Inspired by that good 'hood Chinese food from O.G. Brooklyn, this combo is a little bit Szechuan but without any of the sketchiness of those bulletproof order windows.

3 tablespoons hoisin sauce

2 tablespoons soy sauce

1 tablespoon red pepper flakes

2 garlic cloves, minced

1 (2-inch) piece fresh ginger, peeled and minced

1 pound ground pork

1 teaspoon cornstarch

½ teaspoon black pepper

2 tablespoons vegetable oil

1 pound green beans, trimmed and cut into 1-inch pieces

½ cup salted peanuts

1. In a small bowl, whisk the hoisin sauce, 1 tablespoon of the soy sauce, and the red pepper flakes. Set aside.

2. In a wok or large frying pan, cook the garlic and ginger over medium heat until fragrant, 1 to 2 minutes. Add the pork to the pan and break it up with a wooden spoon. Sprinkle the cornstarch, pepper, and the remaining 1 tablespoon soy sauce onto the pork and cook, stirring, until the pork until is no longer pink, 4 to 5 minutes. Transfer the pork to a bowl. Turn the heat up to high, add the oil and green beans, and cook for 3 minutes, or until the outsides blister.

3. Add the pork and hoisin sauce mixture back to the pan, mix thoroughly, and cook for another minute. Transfer to a platter and garnish with the peanuts.

Better than take-out

THE MAIN LINE

103

FISH FRY

Can we get some condiments up in here?

SERVES 4

- 1½ pounds red snapper fillets, cut into 2-inch pieces
- 2 cups buttermilk
- 2 tablespoons hot sauce, plus more for serving
- 2 cups yellow cornmeal
- 2 teaspoons kosher salt
- 1 teaspoon black pepper
- ½ teaspoon garlic powder
- ½ teaspoon onion powder
- ½ teaspoon cayenne pepper
- 4 cups vegetable oil
- 2 lemons, cut into wedges

Don't let Meghan Markle and her new family in London fool you into thinking that those tea-drinking Englanders have the fried-fish market cornered. You can pay half your rent money to cross the pond for some fish and fries, or pay a subway fare to Brooklyn and go to your cousin and nem's house for a down-home fish fry! And, don't play like you don't know at least one blood relative who fried and sold fish out of their kitchen for a year or more. Maybe you can follow their lead after mastering this recipe!

1. Put the fish in a large bowl, pour over the buttermilk and hot sauce, cover, and marinate in the refrigerator for at least 1 hour and up to 8 hours. Mix the cornmeal, salt, black pepper, garlic powder, onion powder, and cayenne in a shallow plate or bowl.

2. Drain the fish, dredge it in the cornmeal mixture, and place the pieces on a baking sheet. Leave for 5 minutes at room temperature or up to 30 minutes in the refrigerator.

3. Heat the oil in a large, heavy saucepan over medium heat. Add the fish and fry (in batches if needed) for 3 to 4 minutes on each side, until golden brown. Drain on paper towels. Serve with the lemon wedges.

TRAY'S

DINNER PLAYLIST

FEEL ME FLOW, NAUGHTY BY NATURE ■ AIN'T IT FUNNY, J LO AND JA RULE ■ DON'T LET ME DOWN, BIGGIE ■ OLD TO THE NEW, NICE & SMOOTH ■ BATTLEFIELD, JORDIN SPARKS ■ CEREAL KILLER, METHOD MAN & REDMAN ■ WHATTA MAN, SALT-N-PEPA ■ NASTY BOY, BIGGIE ■ GANGSTA'S PARADISE, COOLIO ■ HOW HIGH, METHOD MAN & REDMAN

BOBBY'S BLINGED OUT TACOS

SERVES 4

What's up my cookbook people! If you know me, Bobby, you know I don't do anything unless it's fly as hell! That's why this blinged-out taco would cost you them big bucks if Tray let me serve it on his truck. But, as y'all will soon find out, Tray isn't the only Barker that has that good, good culinary skill. It may have taken me weeks, months, and/or years to perfect, but it's here. Also, that gold is edible. Don't try to cash it at the bank. I learned this the hard way.

FOR THE STEAK

- 2 pounds skirt steak, trimmed
- 1 tablespoon ground cumin
- 1 tablespoon chili powder
- 1 tablespoon kosher salt
- 2 teaspoons black pepper
- ¼ cup olive oil
- ¼ cup soy sauce
- 2 tablespoons white vinegar
- 1 teaspoon honey
- Zest and juice of 1 lime
- Zest and juice of 1 orange

FOR THE TACOS

- 1 cup cooked black-eyed peas
- 1 tablespoon milk
- 1 teaspoon kosher salt
- 4 flour tortillas
- 4 hard shell corn tortillas
- ½ head red cabbage, cored and shredded
- 2 tablespoons pickled onion
- ½ cup chopped fresh cilantro
- ¼ cup cotija cheese
- Edible gold leaf, optional
- 1 small jar pickled jalapeños (optional)

1. To make the steak: Rub the cumin, chili powder, salt, and pepper on the steaks. Cover and rest in the refrigerator for 30 minutes.

2. In a small bowl, whisk the oil, soy sauce, vinegar, honey, lime zest and juice, and orange zest and juice. Place the steaks in a plastic zipper bag, add the marinade, and marinate in the refrigerator for at least 1 hour or up to 4 hours.

3. Heat a grill or large cast-iron frying pan over high heat. Remove the steaks from the marinade and grill them for 3 minutes on each side for rare (125°F), 4 minutes for medium, and 5 minutes for well done.

4. Let the steaks rest for 5 minutes, then slice the meat into 4-inch-long steaks. Rotate them and thinly slice them against the grain. Return the sliced steak to the cooking liquid in the pan.

5. To make the tacos: Combine the black-eyed peas with the salt and milk in a blender or bowl and mash by machine or hand. Set aside.

6. Warm the soft flour tortillas in the microwave by wrapping them in a few wet paper towels and cooking them for 30 to 45 seconds. Keep them wrapped in a tea towel on a plate when serving.

7. Spread 2 tablespoons of the black-eyed pea mixture onto each soft tortilla. Fill each hard taco with layers of the cabbage, steak, pickled onion, cilantro, and cheese. Wrap a soft taco around the exterior of each hard taco, using the bean mixture to adhere. Repeat for the remaining tacos. Top with flakes of edible gold leaf and pickled jalapeños on the side, if using.

MULLINS HOUSE RULES

RULE NO.1: ALL COMMON AREAS NEED TO STAY CLEAN.

RULE NO.2: MAKE UP YOUR BED.

RULE NO.3: NEVER FIND YOURSELF IN TROUBLE.

RULE NO.4: NO PLAYIN' WITH YOUR PLANTAIN.

RULE NO.5: NO FORNICATING AFTER 4.

RULE NO.6: ALWAYS MAKE YOUR CURFEW.

OTHERWISE YOUR'E OUT!

THE BEST VIEW COMES AFTER yours HARD

NEW YORK

SEE THIS PLACE?
THIS IS
MY CASTLE.
I'M THE

GREEN EGGS & SPAM

Is it just me or did Dr. Seuss live in the hood? I've never had Green Eggs and Ham but I've had Green Eggs and Spam. Even better than ham, which will go bad within days, Spam is your buddy through thick and thin. Stock up on some cans and you'll have omelet fixings for years to come.

1 cup frozen spinach, thawed

3 large eggs

¼ cup chopped fresh chives

½ teaspoon kosher salt

¼ can Spam, diced

½ poblano chile, diced

1 garlic clove, minced

1 tablespoon vegetable oil

½ teaspoon black pepper

Hot sauce (optional)

1. Wring out the spinach to get rid of excess water.

2. In a small bowl, beat the eggs with half of the chopped spinach, half of the chives, and the salt. Set aside.

3. In an omelet pan, cook the Spam over medium heat for 2 to 3 minutes. Add the chile and cook for 3 to 4 minutes, until softened. Add the garlic and the rest of the spinach and cook for 2 more minutes, until the garlic is fragrant and sizzling. Transfer the omelet filling to a small bowl.

4. Heat the oil in the pan over medium-high heat. Pour the egg mixture into the pan, swirling the pan to coat all sides. Let it sit for 30 seconds, then swirl the egg around the edges of the pan again. Repeat until the egg no longer moves around. Turn off the heat and add the Spam filling along the center of the egg.

5. Using a spatula, carefully loosen the sides and fold one side over the filling. Loosen the underside of the omelet and roll it over the remaining third of the egg.

6. Transfer to a plate and garnish with the black pepper, the remaining chives, and hot sauce, if using.

GOLDEN FRIED PLANTAINS

First off, let's get this straight: plantains are not bananas! They have a lot more goin' on. When hard and green, they're more savory and good for fritters. Then when they get ripe—with just a few spots of black on the peel—they turn sweet. That's the kind you want to make this dish, which actually originated in Ghana where it is called "kele-wele." I like saying that out loud, over and over, while I'm cooking these.

2 ripe-firm yellow plantains, peeled and sliced diagonally ¼ inch thick

½ teaspoon dried ginger

½ teaspoon onion powder

½ teaspoon cayenne pepper

2 tablespoons coconut oil

1 teaspoon kosher salt

Back Garden Hot Sauce (page 148) for serving (optional)

1. In a large bowl, toss the plantains, ginger, onion powder, and cayenne. Let sit for 5 minutes.

2. Melt the oil in a large nonstick or cast-iron pan over medium heat. Add the plantains and fry for 3 to 5 minutes on each side, until they are browned on the edges. Drain the plantains on a paper towel-lined plate and sprinkle with the salt. Serve with hot sauce if you like.

MILE-HIGH Biscuits

SERVES 8 TO 10

There is nothing quite like a biscuit. Some people look at it as a snack before the main meal. To me it's so much more. A biscuit is a tool: A biscuit can be used to sop up gravy, move vegetables out the way, or sandwich with your favorite fillings (turn the page). If you don't have a biscuit cutter, you can just use a knife to cut the dough into square shapes as shown above.

3 cups all-purpose flour, plus more for dusting

2 tablespoons plus 2 teaspoons sugar

1 teaspoon baking soda

2 teaspoons baking powder

½ teaspoon kosher salt

½ cup (1 stick) cold unsalted butter, plus 1 teaspoon softened butter for the pan

1 cup plus 2 tablespoons buttermilk

1. Set an oven rack to the middle position and preheat the oven to 400°F.

2. In a large bowl, whisk together 2½ cups flour, 2 tablespoons sugar, the baking soda, baking powder, and salt.

3. Dice the ½ cup cold butter. Cut the butter into the flour mixture using a pastry cutter or two butter knives until it is pea-size.

4. Make a well in the center of the bowl, add ½ cup of the buttermilk to the well, and gently fold the buttermilk into the dough using a rubber spatula. Add ½ cup of the remaining buttermilk, taking care not to overwork the dough.

5. Sprinkle a work surface with the remaining ½ cup flour. Transfer the dough to the floured surface and gently knead twice, just until the dough comes together. Roll the dough out to 1-inch thickness. Dust a biscuit cutter with flour and cut out biscuit shapes. Gather the scraps, re-roll them into a disc, and cut once more.

6. Grease a baking sheet with the 1 teaspoon softened butter. Arrange the biscuits on the sheet—it's okay if they touch. Brush the tops of the biscuits with the remaining 2 tablespoons buttermilk and sprinkle with the remaining 2 teaspoons sugar.

7. Bake for 15 minutes, until golden brown. Let cool for 5 to 10 minutes before serving.

KINGS COUNTY
FRIED CHICKEN
(P. 95) WITH
KETCHUP

KINGS COUNTY
FRIED CHICKEN
(P. 95) WITH
MARMALADE

Let's be real, the only thing that doesn't go with biscuits is bullets. Before the Purvis family jacked up Tray's biscuit order on that fateful morning, Tray was on his way to unlocking some of the rarest, yet most delicious, biscuit sandwich combinations. Ranch sauce was just the tip of the iceberg as far as Tray's biscuit genius goes; it only gets better from there!

TRAY'S FAVE
BISCUIT COMBOS

EGG AND
CHEESE WITH
KETCHUP

GREEN EYES'S **FRIED PICKLES** (P. 17) WITH **RANCH** (P. 133)

FRIED SPAM SLICE WITH **CHEESE WHIZ**

RED STRIPED **FRIED SHRIMP** WITH **BUFFALO SAUCE** (P. 70)

TRAY: LEMME ALSO GET FOUR PACKS OF RANCH.
WILLY'S: WHY YOU WANT RANCH? . . . YOU GONNA DUNK THE BISCUITS IN IT?
TRAY: THAT'S MY BUSINESS! JUST PUT IT IN THE BAG.

NOSTRAND AVE STYLE PIGEON PEAS

On Nostrand Ave you can get fresh coconut water too

SERVES 4

Growing up, every other one of our neighbors had island ties, and they made sure to share some of their recipes because they are (rightfully) damn proud of their food. That's where this dish of rice and peas comes in. The coconut milk is what really puts it over the top. Nothing wrong with making a meal out of a pot of these peas.

1 tablespoon olive oil

1 small white onion, chopped

2 garlic cloves, minced

1 tomato, chopped

3 cups cooked pigeon peas, drained

1 cup plus 3 tablespoons coconut milk

1 chicken bouillon cube

1 teaspoon chopped fresh thyme leaves

1 teaspoon paprika

2 scallions, chopped

2 teaspoons kosher salt

2 cups white rice

1. Heat the oil in a Dutch oven or heavy pot over medium-high heat. Add the onion and garlic and cook for 2 to 3 minutes, until browned. Add the tomato and cook for 5 minutes. Add the pigeon peas, coconut milk, bouillon, thyme, paprika, half of the scallions, and salt and bring to a boil. Stir in the rice and boil for 1 minute. Reduce the heat to medium-low and simmer uncovered for 5 minutes.

2. Cover, reduce the heat to the lowest setting, and cook for 20 minutes, until the rice is tender. Fluff the rice with a fork and transfer to a serving bowl. Garnish with the remaining scallions.

ODE to the O.G.

EVERY O.G. KNOWS that the ones who came before him need to be paid their respects. Original Gangsters aren't just gangsters—they can be originators and innovators in their field, or just the baddest ass mothers in their game. We all know that Tray Barker is the Last O.G. of Brooklyn, New York, but what other O.G.s blazed the path for him?

Notorious B.I.G

Talk about an O.G., baby! Biggie needs no introduction. Tray Barker may be the Last O.G., but Biggie is the first.

Barack Obama

America's first Black with a capital "B" President! We salute you, my man!

Michael Jordan

This dude invented basketball, player!

Ol' Dirty Bastard

R.I.P. to the O.G. of the Wu-Tang Clan. He taught the rap game what the game was!

Vito and Michael Corleone

I challenge anyone who said white people didn't have gangs to spend over two hours, three times, with this mob family! That ain't nothing but gang moves right there.

Jackie Gleason

This man taught people how it's possible to laugh your way out of anything, no matter what scary reality might be facing you down. He's the O.G. of comedy.

Michael Jackson

Only a slick mofo can go from being a black man to a white woman and still not be the most surprising member of the family. We ain't forget about you, Jermajesty!

Sidney Poitier

After you guess who's coming to dinner, guess who the flyest guy in Hollywood is.

Jackie Robinson

Mans can bust balls and color lines. Respect!

Humphrey Bogart

In *Casablanca*, with that hat, and that trench, this is an O.G. who knows how to carry himself.

Sammy Sosa

Before he turned white!

STEAMED CABBAGE

Steamed cabbage is like your second cousin in the projects. There's always a pot of cabbage simmering away on the back of the stove. But it was practically a rule to have it at Sunday dinner after church. It may have been the spirit, or my mother's glare, but these were the only vegetables I looked forward to as a kid. Even when I don't go to church, I gotta have me at least one pot of steamed cabbage a week to feel like myself!

1 small white onion, diced

1 tablespoon unsalted butter

1 carrot, peeled and diced

1 habanero chile, minced

1 head green cabbage, cored and coarsely chopped

2 teaspoons black pepper

1 teaspoon kosher salt

1 teaspoon chopped fresh thyme leaves

1. Melt the butter then add the onion and cook 3 to 4 minutes in a Dutch oven over medium heat, until softened. Add the carrot and habanero and cook for 2 minutes. Add the cabbage, pepper, salt, and thyme and cook for 5 to 7 minutes. Add ½ cup water and reduce the heat to medium-low.

2. Cover and cook for 30 to 35 minutes, until the cabbage is translucent and soft.

3. Transfer to a serving bowl and serve.

DOUBLES STYLE CHICKPEAS WITH RICE

In Trinidad they have something called *liming*. It sounds like a culinary term when in fact it is an activity. It is the art of doing absolutely nothing while sharing food and drink. The hearty dish known as *doubles,* a sort of sandwich with a filling of chickpeas and curry, is the perfect way to get your *lime* on. I simplified things by just making the curried chickpeas and serving them over rice.

¼ cup olive oil

2 medium white onions, diced

2 teaspoons kosher salt

1 teaspoon black pepper

4 cups cooked chickpeas, drained

2 cups chicken stock

1 tablespoon curry powder

Juice of 1 lemon

¼ cup chopped fresh flat-leaf parsley

4 cups cooked Carolina Gold rice

1. In a large saucepan, heat the oil over medium heat. Add the onions, salt, and pepper and cook for 4 to 5 minutes, until the onions are softened and browned on the edges. Add the chickpeas and stock and bring to a boil. Cover and cook for 10 minutes, then reduce the heat to low, add the curry powder and lemon juice, and cook, stirring occasionally, for 10 to 15 minutes.

2. Transfer the chickpeas to a serving bowl. Sprinkle the parsley over the top. Serve with the rice alongside.

SIDE PIECES

YOU'RE THE GREATEST Mac & Cheese

2 tablespoons butter, plus more for pan

2 tablespoons all-purpose flour

2 cups milk

1 (4-ounce) package Velveeta Cheese Sauce

1/3 cup shredded pepper Jack cheese

1/4 teaspoon kosher salt

1/4 teaspoon black pepper

1/3 cup shredded extra-sharp Cheddar cheese

1 cup crushed Cheez-Its

8 ounces elbow macaroni

I've gotta break some news to you: Men, if your lady stops baking mac and cheese in the oven, she's just not that into you. You should be as afraid of boxed mac and cheese as you are of a "we need to talk" text or an "I saw your phone" comment. This gesture shows that your lady is no longer willing to address any of your wants in the kitchen, and soon enough that energy will make its way to the bedroom. If this is your journey, do something nice for your darling. Maybe cook this for her for a change.

1. Preheat the oven to 400°F and grease a 9-x-12-inch baking dish.

2. Bring a large pot of water to a boil, salt generously, and add the macaroni. Cook until al dente, then drain.

3. Melt the butter in a large deep skillet or Dutch oven over medium-low heat. Whisk in the flour and continue to whisk for 1 minute, until smooth. Gradually whisk in the milk and continue to cook for 5 minutes, until thickened. Add the Velveeta cheese sauce, pepper Jack cheese, salt, and pepper, then stir in the cooked pasta.

4. Transfer the pasta mixture to the prepared baking dish and top with the Cheddar cheese. Cover with foil and bake for 15 minutes, until golden and bubbly. Remove the foil and sprinkle the Cheez-Its over the top. Bake for another 5 minutes. Let cool for 5 minutes before serving.

SERVES 4

SIDE PIECES

127

Wild Style

YOU MAY NOT KNOW IT, but you've already eaten wild style multiple times in your life. What the hell do you think the first person who made dressing (or as you say, stuffing, Josh!) was thinking? It just took one crazy-ass person to decide to mix together cornbread, turkey juice, and vegetables then throw it in the oven. No, they weren't high off their ass, they were making do with what they had.

Anyone who's been on the inside of a jail cell (or dorm room) especially knows that that jacked up off-brand Dorito at the bottom of the bag topped with week-old mayonnaise and a sprinkle of Lawry's can taste like caviar if it's all you have! More than making do with what's in your pantry or refrigerator, wild style allows you, as the culinary artist, to open up your mind to food possibilities that Iron Chef O.G.s couldn't dream up! If you like chocolate chips and tuna separately, who says they won't make the best damn dip mixed together? Don't let modern day thought ruin your ingenuity! Recipes (except the ones in this book) are the death of the chef. Try it tonight: Mix together three random things you've got in your home, the older the better so you don't waste food, and thank me later.

> **"In prison you gotta be creative. You gotta use every ingredient you can find."**
> **–TRAY**

whatever LEFTOVERS
you have hanging
around in your fridge

some kind of SAUCE—
homemade or not

FRIED EGG—
or over-easy
if you're
feeling queasy

the element of
CRUNCH—
bottom-of-the-bag
chips work well here

SHAY'S SWEET POTATOES

SERVES 6-8

FOR THE SWEET POTATOES
½ cup dried cranberries

½ cup orange juice

2 pounds sweet potatoes, peeled and cubed

½ cup unsweetened nondairy milk

¼ cup brown sugar

1 teaspoon vanilla extract

1 teaspoon ground cinnamon

½ teaspoon kosher salt

4 tablespoons vegan butter

FOR THE TOPPING
¾ cup chopped pecans

⅓ cup instant oats

⅓ cup all-purpose flour

¼ cup brown sugar

½ teaspoon ground cinnamon

½ teaspoon ground ginger

¼ teaspoon kosher salt

2 tablespoons vegan butter, melted

When Shay and Josh told me that they were feeding Shahzad and Amira vegan meals, I thought they were starving the kids to death. Then, they cooked me this. I don't know when, how, or where Shay found the strength to cook without someone dying (see Shay's Repast Spaghetti, page 78), but I don't think I need to know. This woman can feed you soul food that gives you the opposite of the itis. I eat this and I wanna get even more awake, not take a nap!

1. To make the sweet potatoes: Preheat the oven to 350°F. In a small bowl, soak the cranberries in the orange juice for 30 minutes. Bring a pot of water to a boil, add the sweet potatoes and boil for 10 to 12 minutes, until fork tender.

2. In a small bowl, whisk the nondairy milk, brown sugar, vanilla, cinnamon, drained cranberries, and salt. Drain the sweet potatoes and add to the liquid mixture, then transfer to large oblong baking dish (approximately 9 x 13 inches).

3. To make the topping and bake: In a medium bowl, mix all of the topping ingredients together and sprinkle over the sweet potatoes.

4. Dot the topping with the 4 tablespoons of vegan butter and bake for 30 minutes until the topping is golden brown and the sweet potatoes are bubbling.

BROOKLYN
BLOCK PARTY

LISTEN TO ME WHEN I TELL YOU THIS. IF YOU'VE NEVER
BEEN TO ONE, AN AUTHENTIC BROOKLYN BLOCK PARTY WILL CHANGE
THE COURSE OF YOUR LIFE. BACK IN THE DAY, A BLOCK PARTY
WAS LIKE A FAMILY REUNION, BUT WITH THE PEOPLE WHO'D CHECK
YOUR MAIL WHEN YOU'RE OUT OF TOWN. MAYBE YOUR
AUNTIE WOULD ROLL THROUGH BECAUSE SHE USED TO LIVE
ON YOUR BLOCK, BUT OTHER THAN THAT, THIS PRIVATE
AFFAIR IS FOR YOUR CHOSEN FAMILY.

★ AMENITIES ★

JUMP ROPE
When the street is
closed, there's plenty
of room for folks to
show off some fancy
footwork.

LIVE DJ
This is one day of the
year when everybody
can dance in the street.

STOOPS
Stoops are for sitting,
with a brown bag
containing your liquid of
choice, and chilling out
with friends.

OPEN HYDRANT
Who needs a
waterslide?
Get a fireman to ratchet
open one of these and
let the fountain explode.

TRAY'S POTATO SALAD

EVERY BLOCK PARTY NEEDS GOOD POTATO SALAD

During my stint working at the school cafeteria, they had me pushing some bland-ass food. Worst offender: something called "Karen's Potato Salad." Whoever this Karen was, she must have been living a sad colorless existence in a world where the only seasonings were salt and peper. Well, Karen, don't be upset, but I added paprika to your salad. And relish. And a whole bunch of other stuff including the dressing of the gods: Ranch. Now it has become Tray's Potato Salad, a dish I introduced to the public on my food truck at the Taste of Brooklyn Block Party. Now you can bring it to your own block party.

1 tablespoon salt, plus more to taste

1 pound creamer potatoes, peeled and cubed

2 hard-boiled eggs

1 tablespoon relish

2 tablespoons Ranchiest Ranch (see below)

1 teaspoon mustard

2 ribs celery, chopped and leaves reserved

1 teaspoon paprika

SERVES 2

1. Bring a large pot of water to a boil and add the salt. Add the potatoes and boil for 12 to 15 minutes, until fork tender. Drain the potatoes and set aside to cool.

2. Chop one of the hard-boiled eggs and slice the other into rounds. In a large bowl, mix the relish, Ranch, mustard, celery, chopped egg, and paprika. Fold in the potatoes and refrigerate for 1 hour.

3. Taste and adjust the seasoning with more salt, if desired. Garnish with the celery leaves and hard-boiled egg slices.

DOMINOES ARE ALSO ESSENTIAL

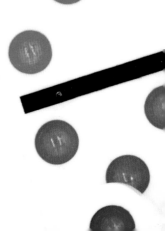

RANCHIEST RANCH

MAKES 1 CUP

1 teaspoon dried dill

1 teaspoon onion powder

1 teaspoon garlic powder

1 teaspoon black pepper

½ teaspoon kosher salt, plus more to taste

½ cup buttermilk

¼ cup mayonnaise

½ teaspoon mustard

1 tablespoon chopped fresh chives

1. Whisk together the dry ingredients in a mixing bowl until fully incorporated. Stir in the buttermilk, mayonnaise, and mustard. Fold in the chives. Taste and add salt if needed.

2. Refrigerate in a jar for up to two weeks. Shake the jar before using.

FRENCH CONNE

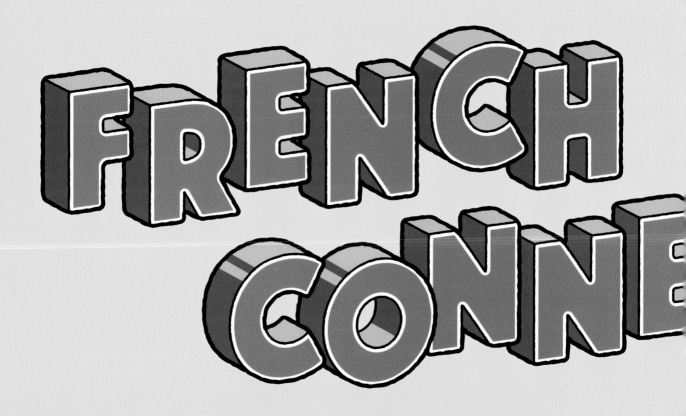

SERVES 4

You won't find any smuggled heroin in these fries, but you will find your new favorite American Idol reboot snack. Straight from the Last Meal on Wheels food truck, these fries are so fancy they may just make you smuggle yourself to France to see if they taste like the real deal. Just make sure you're ready to cut your own potatoes like you would a shiv if you were locked up. Not that I have any experience with that.

FOR THE TOPPING

8 ounces cremini mushrooms, wiped with a paper towel and thinly sliced

½ white onion, chopped

2 garlic cloves, minced

2 tablespoons unsalted butter

1 tablespoon olive oil

1 teaspoon kosher salt

½ teaspoon black pepper

2 tablespoons herbes de Provence

1 cup shredded white Cheddar cheese

FOR THE FRIES

2 pounds russet potatoes, sliced into ¼-inch-thick sticks

1 tablespoon kosher salt, plus more for seasoning

2 cups vegetable oil

CTION FRIES

1. To make the topping: Place the mushrooms in a large dry frying pan over medium heat and cook for 5 to 7 minutes, until they start to sizzle. Add the onion, garlic, butter, and oil and cook for 4 minutes. Add the salt, pepper, and herbs and cook for 8 to 10 minutes, until the mushrooms are browned and the onions are caramelized. Remove from the heat and set aside.

2. To make the fries: Bring a pot of water to a boil and add 1 tablespoon salt. Add the potatoes and boil for 10 minutes, or until tender but not crumbly. Drain the potatoes and pat dry with paper towels.

3. Heat the oil in a large, deep frying pan over medium-high heat. Add the potatoes and fry for 1 minute, nudging them around with tongs or a mesh spider. Drain the fries on a paper towel-lined baking sheet for 30 minutes. At this point, the fries can be frozen and finished another time.

4. Heat the oil back up and fry the potatoes again for 3 to 4 minutes, until golden brown. Drain and sprinkle with salt.

5. To assemble: Preheat the broiler to high.

6. Place half the fries on an oven-safe platter and sprinkle with half of the cheese and half of the mushroom mixture. Add the remaining fries on top and repeat with the remaining cheese and mushroom mixture.

7. Broil for 5 minutes, or until the cheese is melted and bubbling. Serve immediately.

"I GUARANTEE YOUR **FOOT** WILL GO **NUMB.**"

ROSE'S COLLARD GREENS

1 tablespoon vegetable oil

1 large onion, diced

4 garlic cloves, smashed

1 teaspoon kosher salt

1 teaspoon black pepper

2 cups chicken broth

8 ounces smoked turkey, cubed

3 cups stemmed and chopped collard greens

2 cups stemmed and chopped kale

1 tablespoon apple cider vinegar

½ teaspoon sugar

I'm Rose and I'm Tray's mama, Shahzad and Amira's grandmamma, and Shay's worst enemy. Now, I'mma do you like I did my grandbabies and promise you the best collard greens this side of the millenium. I've been making my famous mess of greens since before I could reach the stove as a girl. These have won me awards, and helped me win back my family. Serve it at your next family dinner and let them work their magic. Not that voodoo magic, but that godly magic.

1. Heat the oil in a stockpot or Dutch oven over medium heat. Add the onion, garlic, salt, and pepper and cook for 3 to 5 minutes, until the onions have softened. Add the chicken broth and turkey and bring to a boil. Reduce the heat down to low and add the collard greens and kale. Cover and cook for 45 minutes, stirring occasionally. Stir in the vinegar and sugar and continue to cook for another 15 minutes.

2. Transfer the greens to a serving bowl with some of the cooking liquid and serve.

HOT IN HERRE

Beyoncé isn't the only one who carries hot sauce in her bag. In fact, I make sure I have hot sauce in my pocket wherever I go—because you never know when you might need it. In my opinion, hot sauce will improve just about any kind of food, including the collard greens on this page or the hash browns opposite. But what most folks don't realize is it brings more than heat. It brings depth of flavor, with an underlying acidity. Whether you make your own (see page 148), or just grab a fistful of packets at a fast food joint, try to think of hot sauce as more than a tableside condiment. HERE ARE SOME IDEAS TO GET YOU STARTED:

◆ Stir hot sauce into mayonnaise for a bangin' dip.

◆ Toss hot sauce with still-warm popcorn that will soak it up.

◆ V8 + hot sauce + vodka = Instant Bloody Mary.

◆ Cream hot sauce into butter and slather on corn on the cob.

◆ Make fireball ice pops by mixing lemonade with dashes of hot sauce, then freezing.

It ain't breakfast unless you've got some crispity-crunchity hashbrowns next to that biscuit on your plate! Unlike Karen's potato salad, you don't need to go heavy on the spices to get a beautiful flavor out of these. They're simple and the best addition to any meal. As an added bonus, you don't have to worry about any of the Purvis family shooting you up in a drive-thru!

2 russet potatoes, peeled and grated

1 teaspoon kosher salt, plus more for seasoning

4 teaspoons cornstarch

2 teaspoons onion powder

½ teaspoon cayenne pepper

1 cup vegetable oil

1. Using cheesecloth or a tea towel, squeeze as much water out of the potatoes as you can. Add the salt to the potatoes and let it soak in for 5 minutes. Squeeze again.

2. In a medium bowl, mix together the potatoes, cornstarch, onion powder, and cayenne. Form the potatoes into 4 tight fist-sized balls. Microwave the potatoes for 2 minutes, then let cool.

3. Heat the oil in a large frying pan over medium heat. Carefully place the potato balls into the pan then fry for 3 to 4 minutes on each side, undisturbed, until golden brown.

4. Remove the potatoes from the oil and sprinkle a little salt over them while they are still hot.

O' SO CRISPY HASH BROWNS

SERVES 4

All I Need Cobb Salad

I'll admit, every now and then your boy needs a salad. But, not just any salad that's chopped up with these big knives nowadays. I need one of those salads that makes you feel like you're feeling every tastebud in your mouth. I found out that these existed once I accidentally left Green Eyes in my food truck for too long and he used up all my ingredients for one bowl of God's greatest creation: The Cobb Salad. This salad is for a man with orders from his doctor to eat healthier, or a white woman in Manhattan who doesn't want to get a burger in front of her friends but still wants something real and creamy, like me. This recipe is especially great if you have some eggs hanging out in the back of your fridge that you need to put to use.

1 tablespoon red wine vinegar

¼ teaspoon kosher salt

¼ teaspoon black pepper

1 tablespoon olive oil

1 small shallot, sliced into thin rings

1 avocado, thinly sliced or chopped

2 large eggs

1 boneless chicken breast, cut in half

½ head romaine lettuce, coarsely chopped

¼ wedge iceberg lettuce, coarsely chopped

6 strips turkey bacon, cooked and crumbled

1 cup halved grape tomatoes

¼ cup crumbled blue cheese

2 radishes, thinly sliced

¼ cup Ranchiest Ranch Dressing (page 133)

2 tablespoons finely chopped fresh chives

1. In a small bowl, whisk together the vinegar, salt, pepper, and oil. Add the shallot and avocado and toss lightly.

2. Bring a pot of water to a boil over medium heat. Carefully lower the eggs into the water and boil for 10 minutes. Remove the eggs from the pot and peel under cold running water. Slice the eggs and set aside.

3. Return the water in the same pot to a boil and place the chicken in it. Simmer for 15 to 20 minutes, until it is no longer pink and fully cooked (165°F). Drain, let the chicken cool, then thinly slice it.

4. Spread out the lettuce on a platter or in two salad bowls, then add rows of hard-boiled egg, chicken, turkey bacon, tomatoes, blue cheese, radishes, avocado, and shallots.

5. Drizzle with any remaining oil and vinegar from the vegetables and the ranch dressing and garnish with the chives.

SIDE PIECES

141

FUEGO WATERMELON SALAD

FOR THE HABANERO DRESSING

1 carrot, peeled and chopped

½ red onion, chopped

4 garlic cloves

1 habanero chile, stem removed and halved

2 tablespoons water

Juice of ½ lemon

2 teaspoon kosher salt

1 teaspoon granulated sugar

¾ cup white vinegar

FOR THE SALAD

2 pounds watermelon, rind removed

½ cup crumbled queso fresco

¼ cup mint leaves

2 to 4 tablespoons olive oil

See which one of your little white friends is a real ride or die when they take a bite of this watermelon salad. It starts out so fresh and clean with that melon-mint brightness, then proceeds to whoop your ass with a chile bite that'll make anyone who wasn't raised on a bottle of hot sauce a day really come out of their shell. If the Josh in your life can handle this heat, it's time for you to introduce them to your kitchen. And, I'm talking about the kitchen in your crib—not the one in the back of your head!

1. To make the dressing: In a food processor, combine the carrot, onion, garlic, and chile and pulse into small pieces. Add the water, lemon juice, salt, and sugar and process to a puree. Stir in the vinegar and transfer the dressing to a jar or bottle.

2. To make the salad: Cut the watermelon into cubes or triangles that would fit on a fork and arrrange the watermelon on a platter. Crumble the queso fresco over the watermelon.

3. Spoon 2 tablespoons of dressing over the watermelon and serve the remaining dressing on the side. Garnish the salad with the mint and a drizzle of olive oil.

SHAY'S SWEET & SPICY MANGO SLAW

SERVES 8-10

I'd like to make a disclaimer that this is no substitute for that down-home, dig-your-foot-and-bunion-in-it, mayonnaise-rich cole slaw. But, your girl Shannon is trying to keep these fashionable hips as trim as possible. That's why I came up with this mango slaw as an alternative for the creamier thing. It's worked for me in all settings, meaning my old office or my old neighborhood. I can also trick the kids and Josh into thinking I know how to cook even when someone hasn't died (see my Spaghetti, page 78), which is always a plus!

1 large carrot, peeled

1 ripe mango

4 green onions, finely chopped

1 head red (or green) cabbage, cored and shredded

Zest of 1 lime

1 tablespoon rice vinegar

2 teaspoons Back Garden Hot Sauce (page 148) or storebought

1 teaspoon kosher salt

¼ cup chopped peanuts

1. Using a vegetable peeler, make carrot ribbons by peeling through the entire carrot.

2. Peel the skin from the mango, then use the peeler to peel thin slices of mango.

3. Combine the carrot, mango, green onions, and cabbage in a large bowl. Mix the lime zest, vinegar, hot sauce, and salt in a small bowl. Toss the dressing with the slaw and transfer to a platter.

4. Sprinkle the peanuts on top before serving.

REAL TALK
NUTRITIONAL INEQUALITY

In a 2008 Farm Bill, the USDA defined a food desert as an "area in the United States with limited access to affordable and nutritious food, particularly such an area composed of predominantly lower-income neighborhoods and communities." This means that a group of people—and more often than not, minorities— live in a neighborhood where there is no supermarket and/or very little access to fresh whole foods. They fall back on a reliance on processed foods, convenience stores, and fast food chains to feed their families.

This leads to a diet full of fat, sugar, salt, and preservatives. Consequently, people face a higher risk of morbid obesity, type 2 diabetes, high cholesterol, and other food-related ailments. The problem disproportionately affects black folks, since the phenomenon is largely found in low-income, urban neighborhoods that have been neglected by public services as well as commercial investment. Compounding the problem is the fact that nutritional inequality creates a vicious cycle. A child raised only on processed foods develops a taste only for processed foods and is unlikely to break those habits in later life, then passing them on to the next generation. Though we may think of America as a land of plenty, ironically in the middle of our biggest cities there are millions who have little connection to decent food. Recent studies suggest the roots of the problem may have more to do with socioeconomic forces than with physical location.

But there are points of hope for the future. Across the country, people are taking matters into their own hands and coming up with different ways to address nutritional inequality. For instance, New York has seen a resurgence of community gardens in the past decade. In Brooklyn alone there are now more than two hundred such gardens, which also often serve as gathering places for special events. Often these are founded in abandoned plots of land sandwiched between other buildings. Participants each claim a piece of a raised bed to plant vegetables, fruits, and herbs of their choice.

On a larger scale, there is a new generation of urban farms that have sprouted up in New York and other cities like Chicago and Los Angeles. They may focus on demonstration and education, such as the Youth Farm (pictured opposite). Or, they may focus on commercial harvesting, such as Gotham Greens, a rooftop farm specializing in greenhouse-grown vegetables and herbs.

By coming together, people in every state are working to make healthier food more available. You just have to look around to discover the options, get involved, and maybe just dig into the dirt yourself and get started!

**FOR MORE INFORMATION ON THESE ORGANIZATIONS
AND OTHER SIMILAR ONES, SEE PAGES 216-219.**

HOT SAUCE

MAKES 1 PINT

- 1 pound stemmed fresh chiles, chopped
- 3 tablespoons kosher salt
- 1 teaspoon vegetable oil
- 2 garlic cloves, minced
- 1 onion, chopped
- 2 medium tomatoes, chopped
- 1½ cups distilled white vinegar

Let me tell you, years ago you couldn't tell me that whatever hot sauce was on sale at the bodega wasn't the best hot sauce in the world. But, after playing around in Mullins's kitchen, I stand goddamn corrected! Thanks to these bomb community gardens that have popped up around Brooklyn, I've discovered a whole world of homegrown chiles I didn't know existed—red, orange, green, even black ones. Based on a simple mix of chile peppers, garlic, and tomatoes, this hot sauce will bring the zing to just about any dish. The first step here involves a little bit of bubbly fermentation (which they say is good for your belly too), but you can skip that part if you're short on time.

1. Mix the chiles and salt in a quart-sized jar and cover. Let sit at room temperature for at least 8 hours or up to a full day.

2. Heat the oil in a medium frying pan over medium heat. Add the garlic and cook for 1 to 2 minutes, until fragrant. Add the onion and tomatoes and cook for 5 minutes. Remove from the heat and let cool for 10 minutes.

3. In a food processor or blender, combine the tomato mixture and fermented chiles. Pulse a few times, then let the machine run for 2 minutes. Add the vinegar and process to incorporate. Strain the mixture into a bowl, using a wooden spoon to squeeze out the liquids left in the vegetable solids. Pour the hot sauce into a jar or bottle and store in the refrigerator for up to 2 weeks.

Q&A

WITH

TRACY MORGAN

Between creating and starring in *The Last O.G.* Tracy Morgan is dead-set on changing the way people see Brooklyn and returning citizens. He also wants people to realize that there's more to good pizza than bread and cheese.

Why did you choose to set the show in Brooklyn?

The Last O.G. isn't a show about the community; it's a show starring the community. Brooklyn is the star of the show. It's where I was born and raised. It's where I learned everything I know—both in Brooklyn and the Bronx. My roots are there. If you cut the tree from the roots, what happens to the tree? It dies. That's why I'm never going to forget that I'm rooted in Brooklyn. So many great and important people came out of Brooklyn. It's rich in history. To be a part of that history is important to me.

What makes the food special in Brooklyn?

When I was growing up, we didn't eat *cuisine.* This was old-school Brooklyn, and that's the kind of places I still like—old-school places. I remember there was this special little pizza shop around the corner from where I lived. It had been there since before I was born. The oven in that place musta been more than ninety-five years old. I was practically raised off that pizzeria. It taught me what good pizza should taste like. Since then, I don't eat just anybody's pizza; I ain't never ate chain-restaurant pizza in my life.

If it came off a belt, you ain't gonna get good pizza. Your dough needs to be handmade. I'm specific about who makes my pizza. It's like gettin' a haircut—only certain people can touch my head. Like they say, the secret is all in the sauce. Never go cheap on the sauce. You'll find a lot of places don't like to spend money makin' their sauce. But I'm not gonna eat your pizza if your sauce is trash. Otherwise it's just like eatin' cheese and bread. I don't eat cheese and bread.

What inspired you to come up with *The Last O.G.?*

It's very near and dear to my heart. It came from a vision I had. It's gritty and grimy and dark, but it's also got lots of color. That's how I think of the last O.G.—he's color in a dark place. Back in 2014, after I got hit by that truck, I went through hell. But I ain't come back empty-handed. When I was in that coma, God put this idea in my hands: "Here's *The Last O.G.* for you, bro. A little gift."

How do you see this cookbook working with the show?

All of it starts with education. You'll keep people out of prison if you educate them first. And, it may seem basic, but learning how to cook for yourself and eat properly is part of that education. I hope that through *The Last O.G.* I can give people some support. I just wanna share experiences from my life that everybody can identify and relate to. That's all I wanna do is share that love. By tellin' Tray's story, the things he has to deal with, I'm hoping we can help some people out there who are dealin' with some of the same issues. That's why I'm doing this show.

BODEGA CORN CASSEROLE

It's happened to the best of us: That bae you've been trying to pin down calls you up saying she's ten blocks away and hungry. But you don't have time to run to the grocery store three stops away, so your best option is your corner bodega. If this happens to you, then this corn casserole will change your life. Get the ingredients in a hurry and for under ten bucks. You'll thank me when your lady asks for seconds and a slice of Tray Pie for dessert!

½ cup (1 stick) butter, melted and cooled, plus softened butter for the pan

2 large eggs

1 cup sour cream

1 package Jiffy corn muffin mix

2 cans whole kernel corn, drained

¼ cup jarred pimento peppers

1. Preheat the oven to 375°F and grease a large oblong baking dish (approximately 9 x 13 inches).

2. In a large bowl, whisk the eggs with the butter and sour cream. Mix in the corn muffin mix until smooth. Fold in the corn and pimentos.

3. Transfer to the prepared casserole pan and bake for 35 minutes, until firm in the center. Let cool for approximately 10 minutes before serving.

SERVES 6-8

BODEGA RULES

RULE NO. 1
ORDER QUICKLY

No one wants to wait behind you while you make your mind up on what to order at the bodega. So, come in knowing what you want and order it as quickly as possible so that you can get your slow ass out of there ASAP with a hot meal and no enemies. Bodegas are all about the New York minute—it's a hot minute.

RULE NO. 2
MOVE DOWN TO THE REGISTER

Unless you're dying, do not wait for your sandwich order in front of the counter! Move down to the register, and let someone else order!

RULE NO. 3
RESPECT THE Cat

Any bodega worth its salt will have a cat on patrol. Yes, there may be cat hair or droppings contaminating the space, but who's to say that's unhealthy, huh? The FDA? The CDC? Well, bet money they've never enjoyed a chopped cheese sandwich at 2AM.

AMONG DIE-HARD NEW YORKERS, it's not unheard of to think of the guy behind the counter of your local bodega as a family member. Among the most beloved institutions in any borough, the bodega should be revered, and when you enter, ye shall treat it with the utmost respect, like it's the Vatican of the northeast. From food to Fabulosos to suspect ATMs, bodegas offer it all and are there whenever you need them. If you're unfamiliar, and you'd like to be converted to the nation of Bodega, look no further.

RULE NO. 4

— BE A —
REGULAR

For efficiency's sake, only order the same 1 or 2 items every time you go to your local bodega. This will speed up your process, ingratiate you to the cooks, and possibly save you money, should they decide to slide you your BEC (bacon, egg, and cheese on a roll) free of charge one Sunday morning.

RULE NO. 5

PAY IN
CASH
YOU IDIOT

This ain't Starbucks.

BEHOLD, THE **DESSERT LOAF,** THE SHINING STAR OF MY **PRISON CUISINE!**

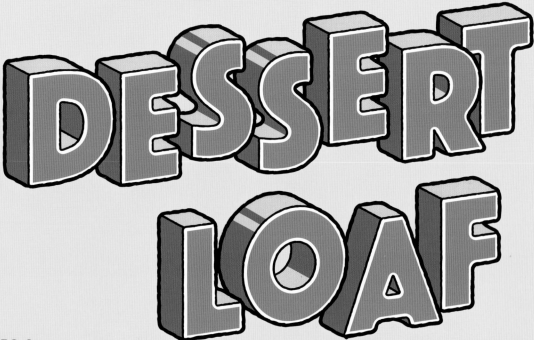

DESSERT LOAF

MAKES 2

FOR THE LOAVES

1 cup (2 sticks) unsalted butter, room temperature, plus more for greasing

½ cup powdered sugar

2 teaspoons Hennessey

½ teaspoon kosher salt

2¾ cups all-purpose flour, plus more for rolling

4 tablespoons Reese's Pieces

½ cup coarsely crushed Original Chex Mix

FOR THE TOPPING

1 (3- to 4-ounce) dark chocolate bar, broken into pieces

2 tablespoons Reese's Pieces

1 cup Original Chex Mix, finely crushed

If I didn't have kids, this dessert loaf would be the greatest creation of my life! Made with a mix of every delicious snack and candy from the commissary, this stuff will surely make your left foot go numb. But it's worth it. Trust me.

1. Preheat the oven to 350°F and grease a baking sheet.

2. In a large bowl or stand mixer, cream the butter and powdered sugar for 1 to 2 minutes. Add the Hennessey, salt, and 1 tablespoon of water and mix until smooth. Add the flour and mix until a stiff dough forms. Stir in the Reese's Pieces and Chex Mix by hand.

3. On a floured surface, divide the dough in half. Roll each half into a smooth log, about 2 inches thick. Place the dough logs on the prepared baking sheet 2 inches apart. Refrigerate for 15 minutes.

4. Place in the oven and bake for 1 hour, until completely dry looking.

5. Cool on the sheet for 15 minutes. The loaves will be very soft at first, but they will harden.

6. Melt the chocolate in the microwave by heating in 10 second bursts and stirring until smooth.

7. Drizzle the loaves with the chocolate and sprinkle on the remaining Reese's Pieces and Chex Mix. Press to adhere the Chex and candy to the chocolate and refrigerate for 30 minutes to set. Remove from the refrigerator and let the loaves rest, covered in an airtight container, for at least four hours and up to one day. (This resting period is necessary so that the loaves will slice well and not crumble.) Use a serrated knife to slice into ½-inch-thick cookies.

SWEET STUFF

HOTEP BEAN PIE

Bean pie is kissin' cousins with sweet potato pie.

SERVES 8

- 2 tablespoons all-purpose flour, plus more for rolling
- 1 store-bought pie crust
- 2½ cups cooked navy beans, drained
- 1½ cups evaporated milk
- 4 large eggs
- ¾ cup granulated sugar
- 2 tablespoons brown sugar
- ¼ cup (½ stick) unsalted butter, melted
- 2 teaspoons ground cinnamon
- 2 teaspoons vanilla extract

162

This pie will not be served with a side of suspect facts linking it back to Africa, but it will bring you down to your Kunta Kinte Roots! We're taking it old school, inspired by the single-serving baby pies that my Nation of Islam brothers sell all around Bed Stuy even today. Have a slice of this and you'll feel like a true Brooklynite. To take it to the next level, serve with a dollop of whipped cream.

1. Preheat the oven to 350°F.

2. On a lightly floured surface, roll out the pie crust so it is a little bigger than your 9-inch pie plate. Place it in a 9-inch pie plate and cover it with a sheet of parchment paper. Weigh it down with pie weights or dried beans and bake for 20 to 25 minutes, until the edges are lightly browned. Remove from the oven and cool completely.

3. In a blender or food processor, combine the flour, navy beans, evaporated milk, eggs, granulated and brown sugars, butter, cinnamon, and vanilla and blend until smooth.

4. Strain the mixture into the crust and discard the solids. Bake for 45 to 50 minutes, until the center is set. Let cool for 10 to 15 minutes before slicing.

Peanut Butter Cornbread

When I started working at Grundle's, I found out that people love to eat scones, but those are some crumbly-ass, useless pastries! What happened to good old-fashioned cornbread? You can eat it morning, noon, and night—always satisfying. I wanted to introduce Shahzad and Amira to cornbread, as part of their cultural inheritance. But I knew I'd have to ease them into it. That's why I tricked it out by adding Reese's Pieces. But you don't need to go that far. Instead, try this recipe with peanut butter swirled in the batter and crushed peanuts on top for crunch.

6 tablespoons (¾ stick) unsalted butter

½ cup crushed salted peanuts

½ cup brown sugar

1¼ cups fine cornmeal

½ cup all-purpose flour

1 teaspoon baking powder

1 teaspoon kosher salt

2 large eggs

1½ cups whole milk

6 tablespoons smooth peanut butter

1. Set an oven rack to the middle position and preheat the oven to 400°F.

2. Place the butter in a 10-inch cast-iron pan, place the pan in the oven, and let the butter melt, 2 to 3 minutes.

3. In a small bowl, mix the crushed peanuts with 1 tablespoon of the brown sugar. Set aside. In a large bowl, whisk the cornmeal, flour, baking powder, remaining brown sugar, and salt. In a medium bowl, whisk together the eggs, milk, melted butter, and peanut butter until smooth. Add the liquid mixture to the dry ingredients and whisk until fully combined.

4. Transfer the batter to the buttered cast-iron pan. Sprinkle the peanut topping over the batter. Bake for 38 to 40 minutes, until a knife inserted in the center comes out clean.

5. Remove from the oven and let cool for 10 to 15 minutes before slicing into wedges.

PBJ BEIGNETS

FOR THE JELLY FILLING

¾ cup jelly (grape or your choice)

2 tablespoons warm water

FOR THE PEANUT BUTTER GLAZE

6 tablespoons creamy peanut butter

2 tablespoons unsalted butter

2 tablespoons confectioners' sugar

1 tablespoon evaporated milk

½ teaspoon vanilla extract

FOR THE BEIGNETS

¾ cup lukewarm water

¼ cup sugar

1 teaspoon active dry yeast

1 large egg, lightly beaten

½ teaspoon kosher salt

½ cup evaporated milk

3½ cups bread flour, plus more for rolling

2 tablespoons shortening

Nonstick cooking spray

3 cups vegetable oil

1½ cups confectioners' sugar

Yo, ain't nothing better than a good old-fashioned peanut butter and jelly sandwich. Two of the greatest spreads in the world coming together to create an unstoppable and timeless combination! Whether you're a kid or an adult, you may feel like your mouth may never unstick itself from the insane amount of peanut butter you spread on that mug, but the experience is worth it. That's why I had to make it a little fancier and bring some of that Nawlins' swag into this bad boy. Yep, these are the world's greatest PBJ Beignets. If people can eat burgers on donuts, then I can eat a fried PB&J sandwich!

1. To make the jelly filling: In a small bowl, whisk the warm water with the jelly.

2. To make the peanut butter glaze: Combine all the ingredients in a small saucepan over low heat and cook for 2 to 3 minutes, whisking until smooth.

3. To make the beignets: In a large bowl, combine the lukewarm water, sugar, and yeast. Let it bloom for 10 minutes. Whisk the egg, salt, and evaporated milk into the yeast mixture. Add the bread flour 1 cup at a time and stir until it forms a ragged dough. Stir the shortening into the dough.

4. Lightly flour a work surface and knead the dough until it forms a smooth ball. Spray a large bowl with cooking spray and place the dough in it. Cover with plastic wrap and let rest in a warm place for 2 hours.

5. Once the dough has risen, roll it out on a floured surface to ¼-inch thickness. Cut out 2-x-1-inch rectangles. Gather the scraps and knead into a smooth ball, then roll out again (the second rolling avoids irregular folds). Let the dough rest for 10 minutes.

6. Meanwhile, heat the oil in a large deep frying pan over medium heat to 375°F. Working in batches to avoid crowding the pan, add the beignets and fry for 3 to 4 minutes on each side, until they float and turn golden brown. Remove the beignets to a paper towel–lined plate.

7. Using a piping bag, zipper bag, or squeeze bottle, drive the opening into each beignet and fill with 1 teaspoon of the jelly filling. Reheat the peanut butter glaze and glaze the beignets. Using a sieve, dust the beignets with the powdered sugar.

FALLEN ANGEL CANNOLI

2 cups ricotta cheese

¾ cup powdered sugar, plus extra for dusting

Juice of 1 lemon

¼ cup finely chopped milk chocolate, plus more for topping

1 teaspoon ground cinnamon

½ teaspoon ground allspice

8 sugar cones

¼ cup chopped pecans

I'mma be honest, my recipe says this makes 8 servings, but best believe it's really just 1 because you'll eat these up before you can even put them on a plate—which is good in a way because these need to be eaten real quick after they're made. No one likes cheese that's been sitting out too long. Be kind to yourself and your guests, okay!

1. Place the ricotta cheese in a strainer nested in a bowl and drain for 1 hour. Discard the excess whey.

2. Transfer the ricotta cheese to a small bowl and mix in the sugar, lemon juice, chocolate, cinnamon, and allspice. Chill for 1 hour.

3. Scoop ¼ cup of the filling into each cone. Garnish with the pecans, sifted powdered sugar, and more chocolate.

SWEET STUFF

166

PROPS TO
The Godfather

JUST ASK TRAY, if you watch *The Godfather*—all three movies—you'll have everything you need to know about life. Money has its place and so does respect. But you can have all the money in the world and the ultimate respect, but you have nothing without your family.

"I'm gonna make him an offer he can't refuse." —VITO CORLEONE

Whether that offer is to ask Mullins on a fake double date so that you can extend your halfway house curfew, or allowing Green Eyes to work on your food truck for minimum, minimum wage, make sure your offers to both your friends and enemies are bulletproof.

"Don't ever take sides with anyone against the family again. Ever." —MICHAEL CORLEONE

No matter how much of a stupid ass Cousin Bobby may be, you'll never catch Tray tossing his big mouth to the curb. Even Shay forgave Tray; he's family after all.

"Friendship is everything. Friendship is more than talent. It is more than the government. It is almost the equal of family." —VITO CORLEONE

Even if those friends land you in jail, Clyde, make sure you've got real ones who will help you plan a failed murder attempt just because they love you.

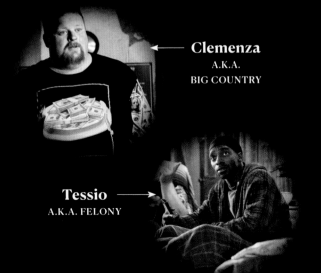

Clemenza
A.K.A.
BIG COUNTRY

Tessio
A.K.A. FELONY

HEAVEN BOUND
COCONUT CAKE

MAKES 2 LOAF CAKES

My Mama Rose never let a Sunday go by without making this cake. She'd sell it at church to convince old-time members and newcomers that a slice of this coconut cake would send them on an even more direct flight to heaven than paying their tithes! Mama had game, and she knew just how to keep butts in church seats with her drug of choice, cake.

1. To make the glaze: In a medium bowl, whisk the powdered sugar and coconut water until smooth. Add the coconut flakes and set aside.

2. To make the cake: Preheat the oven to 325°F. Grease a 9-inch Bundt pan or two loaf pans and dust with flour.

3. In a large bowl or stand mixer, cream the butter with the cream cheese and granulated sugar. Add the eggs one at a time. Gradually sift the flour into the batter 1 cup at a time. Add the coconut milk and vanilla and stir until smooth.

4. Bake for 1 hour and 30 minutes, until a toothpick inserted in the center comes out clean. Remove from the oven and let cool for 30 minutes.

5. Dislodge the cake by running a butter knife around the edges. Place the cake on a platter and drizzle the glaze over it. Let set at room temperature for 1 hour, then garnish with maraschino cherries.

FOR THE GLAZE

2 cups powdered sugar

¼ cup coconut water

2 tablespoons coconut flakes

FOR THE CAKE

1 cup (2 sticks) unsalted butter, room temperature, plus more for greasing the pan

3 cups all-purpose flour, plus ¼ cup to coat the pan

1 cup cream cheese, room temperature

3 cups granulated sugar

6 large eggs

¼ cup coconut milk

1 teaspoon vanilla extract

Maraschino cherries for garnish

SWEET STUFF

169

SERIOUS CEREAL

The one crime you'll never get locked up for is being a cereal killer. The diet of champions, cereal is the culinary genius's infallible mix-in. In fact, If the wildest thing you've done with cereal is pour milk first and then add the cereal, you're doing it wrong. Cereal can, and should be, used for just about every meal.

COCOA PUFFS

Crank up your breakfast with these in The Goods Muffins (page 173)

GOLDEN GRAHAMS

Bash these up, then dust over your buttered French toast or pancakes—you won't event need the syrup.

FRUIT LOOPS

Give these to a kid with some yarn and you got a craft project that will last for hours.

FROSTED FLAKES

Crumble up the flakes and add to seasoned flour for breading fried chicken.

COCOA KRISPIES

Remember "ants on a log"? Make it your way by spreading peanut butter on celery sticks and dotting with Krispies.

LUCKY CHARMS

When you get to the end of the box: Pour out the remains, count each type, and play those numbers in lotto.

CORN POPS

Sprinkle these on top of butter pecan ice cream.

BIG COUNTRY'S TURTLES

SERVES 6-8

It's Big Country. I don't know nothing about no food you can't take out of a wrapper, but I accidentally mixed all of these things in my mouth once and thought the combo was kind of fantastic.

24 ounces peanut brittle
16 soft caramel candies
1 tablespoon milk
½ cup milk chocolate chips

1. Line a baking sheet with parchment paper and spread the peanut brittle out into a single layer.

2. In a small saucepan, melt the caramels with the milk over low heat, whisking for 3 to 4 minutes, until smooth. Drizzle the caramel over the peanut brittle.

3. Add the chocolate to the same saucepan with the heat off and stir to melt. If the chocolate does not melt, place the pan back over low heat for 30 seconds, take it off the heat, and stir. Repeat until smooth. Pour the chocolate over the peanut brittle and caramel.

4. Chill the brittle in the fridge for 30 minutes, or until hardened. Break the brittle up into bite-size pieces.

THE GOODS

MUFFINS

The only goods I'm selling nowadays are legal and delicious. Stop by my food truck for breakfast and you'll be served up these sweet, salty, and wild-style muffins that'll be the perfect start to your day. When you make these yourself, your kids may wonder where all their food went in the house, but you just tell them to stay out of grown folks business and eat their muffin!

SERVES 12

2 cups all-purpose flour

1¼ cups light brown sugar

⅔ cup Ovaltine

1 teaspoon baking powder

1 teaspoon baking soda

¾ teaspoon kosher salt

2 large eggs

¾ cup milk

2 teaspoons vanilla extract

2 teaspoons white or apple cider vinegar

½ cup (1 stick) unsalted butter, melted and cooled

½ cup chocolate chips

½ cup Cocoa Puffs

½ cup M&M's

1. Preheat the oven to 350°F. Place 12 paper liners in the wells of a muffin pan.

2. In a large bowl, combine the flour, brown sugar, Ovaltine, baking powder, baking soda, and salt. In a smaller bowl, whisk together the eggs, milk, vanilla, vinegar, and butter. Add the wet ingredients to the dry ingredients and stir to combine. Fold in the chocolate chips.

3. Ladle the batter into the prepared muffin pan, filling each cup three quarters full. Top each muffin with Cocoa Puffs and M&M's, pressing down lightly. Bake for 25 minutes, or until a toothpick inserted in the center comes out clean. Let cool for 10 minutes before serving.

LEMON DROPS

There was a short time—that I ain't proud of—when I started backsliding and selling crack again, with my cuzzo Bobby. To reach out to a new clientele, we rebranded our product as "Lemon Drops." Now I know we were wrong. This is my way of saying sorry. These perfectly legal treats are sweet, a little tart, and definitely addictive—in a good way. Enjoy!

1 cup (2 sticks) unsalted butter, at room temperature

½ cup powdered sugar

1 teaspoon limoncello

¼ teaspoon lemon extract

½ teaspoon kosher salt

2 teaspoons lemon zest

2¼ cups all-purpose flour

FOR THE TOPPING

1 cup powdered sugar

⅓ cup limoncello

½ cup crushed shelled pistachios

1. To make the lemon drops: Preheat the oven to 350°F.

2. Cream the butter and powdered sugar in a mixing bowl or stand mixer for 1 to 2 minutes. Add the limoncello, lemon extract, and salt and mix until smooth. Add the lemon zest and flour and mix until a stiff dough forms.

3. Using a small ice cream scooper, scoop out batter rounds and place them 1 to 2 inches apart on an ungreased cookie sheet. Bake for 10 to 12 minutes, until they no longer look wet. Cool for 10 minutes. They will be very soft at first, but they will harden as they cool.

4. To make the topping and assemble: In a small bowl, whisk the powdered sugar with the limoncello.

5. Drizzle each cookie with the icing, then sprinkle the pistachios on top. Let stand for 10 to 15 minutes for the icing to set.

6. Store the cookies in an airtight container for up to 3 days or freeze for up to 1 month.

SWEET STUFF

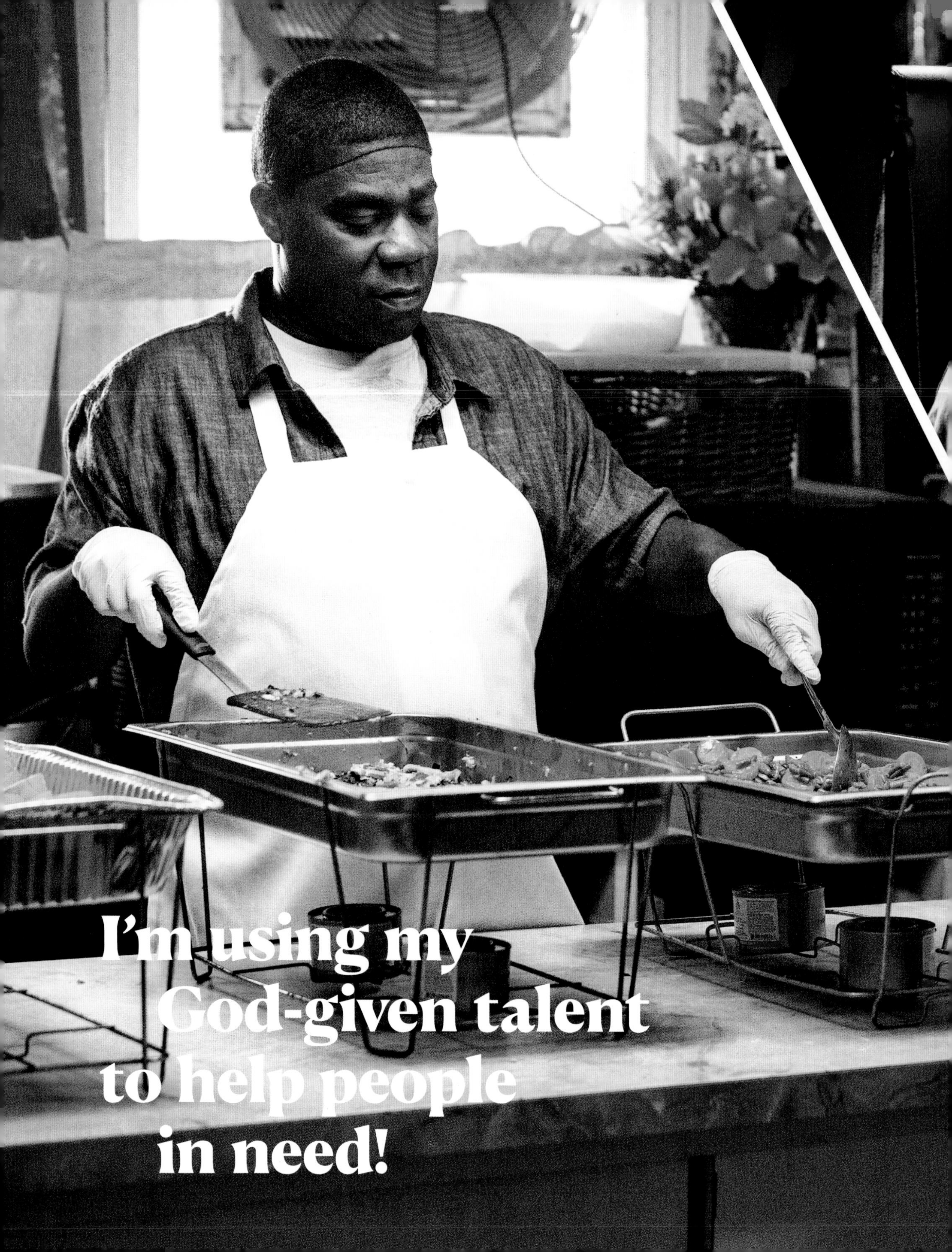

I'm using my
God-given talent
to help people
in need!

PRISON CHEESECAKE

SERVES 8-10

You don't have to be in prison to enjoy this cheesecake, which might leave the folks at Junior's quivering in fear. Simple and delicious, it can be made in the oven or with a microwave. It's also great with a crust made from Nilla Wafers or Oreos!

1 (6-ounce) package graham crackers

5 tablespoons margarine

6 Mini Babybel snack cheeses

¼ cup lemon juice

4 vanilla Jell-O pudding cups

1. Crush the graham crackers in a zipper bag or pulse in a food processor until they form fine crumbs. Mix in the margarine. Press flat into a glass pie dish.

2. Either bake the crust in the oven or microwave. Oven method: Preheat the oven to 350°F. Bake for 6 to 8 minutes, until firm and not squishy. Microwave method: Cook for 1 to 2 minutes. Let cool.

3. Using a whisk in a bowl or in a food processor, soften the cheese with the lemon juice until it becomes a smooth paste. Gradually add the vanilla pudding.

4. Transfer the pudding to the graham cracker crust. Cover with plastic wrap and chill in the refrigerator for at least 4 hours to set. (It will keep, covered in the refrigerator, for up to 1 day.) Slice and serve.

SWEET STUFF

REAL TALK

RE-ENTRY

The effects of incarceration go far beyond the prison cell. Once a person has a criminal record, the basics of day-to-day life in society—such as getting a job and finding housing—become all the more difficult. Considering how inhospitable the outside world can be for former inmates, it's no wonder the rate of recidivism is so high: roughly three-quarters of ex-prisoners are arrested again within five years.

Studies have shown that finding a job soon after release from prison can reduce the rate of relapse into criminal activity by 20 percent. And yet, a criminal record reduces the likelihood of a job offer by nearly 50 percent. Many attempts are being made to resolve this discrepancy: from "ban the box" campaigns that strive to remove questions about criminal records from job applications to programs that aim to match former inmates with jobs.

Employment isn't the only hurdle people face after being released. In the close quarters of a prison, infectious diseases such as tuberculosis, Hepatitis B and C, and HIV/AIDS are incredibly common. Many leave prison with health concerns they didn't have when they were admitted—and, combined with already strained finances, these can be debilitating.

A strong social support system can help offset some of the problems newly released inmates face. In fact, studies find a strong correlation between community ties and successful reentry for ex-prisoners. However, maintaining relationships with family and community while in prison can be extremely difficult. Policies around visitation vary widely by state: North Carolina, one of the stricter states, allows for only one two-hour visit per week. Across nearly all prisons, visits are considered a "privilege" that can be taken away, and phone calls are much more expensive than in the outside world. Advocating for increased visitation rights for prisoners is one of many ways you can help.

FOR MORE INFORMATION ON ORGANIZATIONS WHERE YOU CAN GET INVOLVED TO HELP, SEE PAGES 216-219.

BROOKLYN KNOCK-OUT SUNDAE

RECIPE CONTINUES

SERVES 2-4

LL Cool J's mama may have told him to knock you out, but the only thing I want to knock out of you are your taste buds! This badass chocolate chunk of a seriously delicious treat will knock your socks off.

2 tablespoons store-bought hot fudge sauce

1 scoop chocolate ice cream

1 scoop vanilla ice cream

1 (2-inch) square brownie, cubed

¼ cup chopped pecans

1 scoop butter pecan ice cream

¼ cup large milk chocolate chips

Whipped cream, for topping

2 cherries, pitted and split in half

1 teaspoon chocolate sprinkles

1. In a bowl, heat the fudge in the microwave for 40 seconds. Stir to smooth it out.

2. Scoop the chocolate ice cream into a dish. Dip the scoop in hot water to clean it quickly, then scoop the vanilla ice cream next to the chocolate.

3. Layer the brownie over the two scoops and sprinkle half of the pecans over it.

4. Dip the scoop in the water one more time and scoop on the butter pecan ice cream.

5. Pour the hot fudge over the ice cream and sprinkle on the remaining pecans and the chocolate chips. Top the ice cream with whipped cream, the cherries, and sprinkles.

Food fight!

SPREAD THE LOVE BROWNIE

MAKES 40 TO 42 MINI-CUPCAKES

Nonstick cooking spray

½ cup all-purpose flour, plus more for dusting

10 tablespoons unsalted butter, room temperature

¾ cup granulated sugar

½ cup brown sugar

¾ cup unsweetened cocoa powder

2 teaspoons vanilla extract

½ teaspoon salt

2 large eggs

½ cup chopped dark chocolate

1. Preheat the oven to 350°F. Grease a mini cupcake pan with a generous amount of cooking spray and dust with flour.

2. Cream the butter with the granulated and brown sugars in the bowl of an electric mixer until fluffy, about 5 minutes. Add the cocoa powder, vanilla, and salt and mix until combined. Blend in the eggs, one at a time, until fully incorporated. Stir in the flour until it is no longer visible, then fold in the chopped chocolate.

3. Roll 2 tablespoons of batter into a smooth ball and place it in a cupcake well. Repeat with the remaining batter.

4. Bake for 12 to 15 minutes, until the brownie centers are set and a knife comes out clean. Let the brownies cool in the pan for 10 minutes. Use a butter knife to loosen the edges of the brownies, remove from the pan, and let rest for 10 minutes on a cooling rack.

AMIRA'S *Peach Cobbler*

SERVES 6-8

So, unlike Shahzad, I've been given oven access since I could stand on my two feet. And, since then, I've curated a wonderful menu of dishes should I ever be left on my own. Of these dishes, my peach cobbler is an obvious winner. Even all of the white girls at school love it, and don't even ask to have it with Cool Whip or ice cream. It's that good, not to toot my own horn or anything, but seriously, "toot toot," because I've never even seen a contestant on *The Great British Bakeoff* come close to perfecting this classic. Be sure to eat it cozied up to the window while reading one of the great novels of our time. Anything Toni Morrison will be a great fit.

¾ cup all-purpose flour, plus more for dusting

¼ cup cornmeal

¾ cup granulated sugar, plus 3 tablespoons for sprinkling

¾ teaspoon kosher salt

6 tablespoons (¾ stick) cold unsalted butter, cut into chunks

1 large egg yolk

1 large egg

4 cups frozen sliced peaches

1 cup fresh blackberries

2 teaspoons lemon juice

1½ teaspoons cornstarch

1. Combine the flour, cornmeal, ¼ cup of the sugar, and ½ teaspoon of the salt in a large bowl. Cut the butter into the flour mixture using a cold pastry cutter, two knives, or your hands until the butter chunks are pea-size.

2. Make a well in the center of the batter, add the egg yolk and 1 tablespoon ice water, and mix to form a sticky dough. Transfer the dough to a sheet of plastic wrap dusted with flour. Wrap it and chill in the refrigerator for 1 hour.

3. Preheat the oven to 325°F.

4. In a small bowl, whisk together the whole egg with 1 teaspoon water. Set aside.

5. In a large bowl, combine the peaches, blackberries, lemon juice, cornstarch, the remaining ½ cup sugar, and ¼ teaspoon salt. Stir well. Transfer the fruit mixture to an 9-x-13-inch baking dish.

6. Roll out the pastry dough onto a floured surface to ¼-inch thickness. Cut the dough into 1-inch strips and carefully place them over the fruit. Brush the pastry with the egg wash.

7. Bake the cobbler for 40 minutes, until the crust is golden and the filling is bubbling, then remove the cobbler from the oven and sprinkle the remaining 3 tablespoons sugar over it. Let cool for 10 to 15 minutes before serving.

SWEET STUFF

187

GREEN MILE

FOR THE GINGER SIMPLE SYRUP

1 cup granulated sugar

1 cup water

4 ounces fresh ginger, peeled and chopped

FOR THE GREEN MILE

1 cup pineapple juice, chilled

12 ice cubes

2 teaspoons matcha powder

2 tablespoons ginger simple syrup (see above)

Having this drink won't kill you, like it might in Louisiana, but this juice with green powder, that I've since learned is "matcha," will give you the energy of a solitary inmate that just got his first taste of the outdoors in fifteen years. Inspired by the only prison film worth watching, *Green Mile* (they were more robbed for that Best Picture Oscar in 2000 than Faith was when Lisa and Shay rolled up trying to steal her couch!), this pineapple matcha tea drink will make you feel fancy and smart.

1. To make the simple syrup: In a small saucepan, combine the sugar and water and bring to a boil, stirring to dissolve the sugar. Add the ginger and simmer for 1 minute. Remove the pan from the heat and steep, covered, for 30 minutes to 1 hour. Strain and store in an airtight container or bottle in the fridge.

2. To make the Green Miles: Put 4 ice cubes and ¼ cup of the pineapple juice into each of two glasses. Sift the matcha powder into a cocktail shaker. Pour the remaining ½ cup pineapple juice and the ginger simple syrup into the shaker. Close and shake vigorously. Add the rest of the ice to the shaker and shake for 1 minute. Strain the matcha mixture into each glass.

GRUNDLE'S
GARVEY PALMER

One of the first things I did when I got hired at Grundle's was celebrate Black History Month. No, it wasn't February, but Wavy was out here running an establishment whiter than Josh's ass! To show him and Elizabeth that black culture was alive and very well, I taught them about my favorite black person besides myself, Marcus Garvey. My man had that Jamaican heritage that made him cooler than Bob Marley and all his sons mixed together. Plus, he advocated for all kinds of black people, and that's the type of man I wanna be. If one of us comes up, we all do! After my short, but informative, lesson, Grundle's has served this coffee drink (off menu) ever since! Long live the sort of King of Blackness!

4 cups brewed coffee, cooled · 2⅔ cups lemonade

¼ cup almond milk

1. Pour the coffee into ice cube trays and freeze overnight.

2. In the morning, add 4 to 6 coffee ice cubes to each of four glasses. Pour ⅔ cup lemonade over each serving. Or for 8 smaller servings, add 2 cubes per ⅓ cup of lemonade.

3. Finish each glass with a splash of almond milk.

66

Coffee is my
NEW
HUSTLE.
–WAVY

MAKES
4 OR 8

ORANGE AND BLUE JUICE

When I went away, y'all may have made that Purple Drank the beverage of choice, but I've got something even better. Back in the day, I made this mix every New York Knicks game day in 2000 and 2001. And guess what? They had some of their best seasons ever. That's because even if I'm not paying my good money for some overpriced arena tickets, you better believe me and my Shay Shay were drankin' that good orange and blue juice every game day! Mix this drink, watch those colors mingle in the glass, and focus your energy on the game, because the Knicks will rise again!

8 cups mango nectar

4 cups orange juice

1 cup frozen blueberries

SERVES 8

1. Stir the mango nectar and orange juice in a large pitcher. Pour the juice into a glass. Garnish each glass with two tablespoons of the frozen blueberries and stir slightly to make blue swirls.

PINEAPPLE ICE

SERVES 4

Nothing better than a pineapple drink that'll make you feel like you're on a beach, or at least looking at one in a magazine. Tastes fresh, and even if you get your pineapple juice from the deli, you'll never be able to tell because of the added honey and lime. And, don't tell anyone I told you, but if you want to add a little somethin', somethin' like vodka, I won't snitch on you!

3 limes

2 cups pineapple juice

2 tablespoons honey

1. Cut two wheels from a lime, cut them in half, and refrigerate until ready to serve.

2. Zest the limes and juice them (you should have ¼ cup of juice).

3. Whisk the pineapple juice, lime juice, and honey in a medium bowl. Pour the juice mixture into a shallow baking dish and freeze for at least 4 hours, until firm.

4. Remove the dish from the freezer and run a fork through the ice to break it up. Cover and freeze for another 3 hours, or until firm.

5. To serve, scoop into dessert dishes or glasses and garnish with half a lime wheel.

MAGIC DUST

RED KOOL-AID

Back in the day, every neighborhood had something called "the Kool-Aid house." That was the place where all the kids (and a lot of the adults) wanted to congregate. In the center of the kitchen table always sat a fat jug of red Kool-Aid—one that seemed to magically refill itself. It was an open invitation for anybody to step inside and chill out for a while. By the way, if you didn't know it already, red is a flavor as well as a color.

GRAPE KOOL-AID

A close second to red, grape flavor is equally versatile, sort of like a house wine. Maybe that's why it feels a little more adult, especially if you serve over ice with a lemon wedge garnish. It pairs best with classic savory dishes such as mac 'n' cheese (page 127).

ORANGE KOOL-AID

There's no need to buy food coloring if you have Kool-Aid around. You can use it to make icing: Add just enough water to dissolve, then beat with powdered sugar. Try this with orange flavor to spread atop The Goods Muffins (page 173) for a trippy treat for Halloween.

GREEN APPLE KOOL-AID

Green apple is probably the tartest flavor in the Kool-Aid arsenal, and that makes it an ideal refresher. Mix a batch then freeze and break up following the technique of Pineapple Ice (page 197) for a fancy little dish to cleanse your palate between courses.

"I'M GONNA BUST IN THERE LIKE THE KOOL-AID MAN!"
—SHAY

THE last OG.

JOSH'S RECOVERY SMOOTHIE

2 cups unsweetened almond milk

½ cup instant oats

2 ripe bananas, broken into chunks and frozen

¼ cup almond butter

1 teaspoon honey

2 ice cubes

2 dashes of ground nutmeg

Josh here. Tray's asked me to come up with a "fire as f*ck recipe" for his cookbook that I doubt will ever hit shelves, or maybe it will given that I'm now involved. Moreover, Tray explicitly told me not to sour this book with any "corporate, bland, yuppie, kale-type shit," but according to my Instagram followers, this smoothie is "the shit," as the kids would say. Whether you need to recover from your wife's ex and baby father's nonstop communication or you've just run a NYC marathon, this smoothie is the drink for you. Recover from whatever ails you in life with this vegan smoothie that tastes better than homemade banana bread. Well, it might if you haven't had banana bread in decades, like me.

1. Put the almond milk and oats in a blender and let them soak for 5 minutes. Add the bananas, almond butter, honey, and ice and pulse a few times to break them down, then blend on low speed for 2 minutes until smooth.

2. Pour the smoothie into two glasses and garnish with the nutmeg.

"I wasn't thrilled when you showed up, but I was wrong"

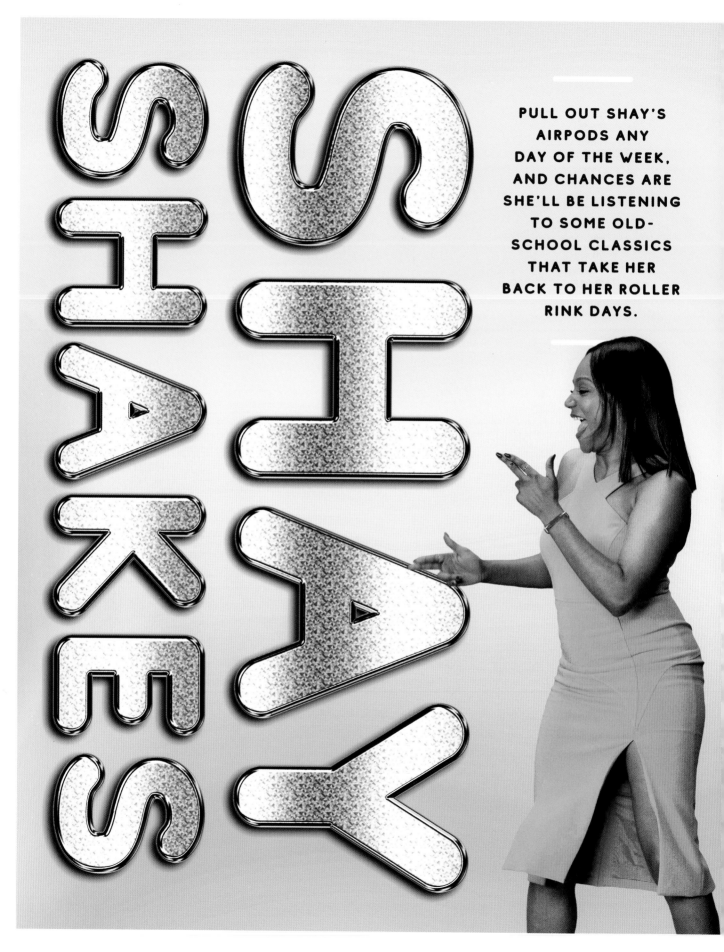

SHAYS SHAKES STAY

PULL OUT SHAY'S AIRPODS ANY DAY OF THE WEEK, AND CHANCES ARE SHE'LL BE LISTENING TO SOME OLD-SCHOOL CLASSICS THAT TAKE HER BACK TO HER ROLLER RINK DAYS.

I WILL ALWAYS LOVE YOU, Whitney Houston

NO SCRUBS, TLC

MMMBOP, Hanson

"Damn! Who knew these three little white boys could make fake words sound so sexy!"

KILLING ME SOFTLY, Lauryn Hill

SAY MY NAME, Destiny's Child

STACY'S MOM, Fountains of Wayne

WHO'S THAT GIRL, Eve

"I'll never show you, but you know how Eve has those two paw prints tattooed on her chest? Well I have two of my own. You just can't see 'em."

RIGHT THURR, Chingy

CRY ME A RIVER, Justin Timberlake

HARD KNOCK LIFE, Jay-Z

"This is a hood anthem right here! The only man I would have left Tray for is Jay-Z, and bet I still could get him away from Beyoncé!"

FALLIN', Alicia Keys

WAVY'S FLAVA

SERVES 2

All these years of running Grundle's and I never got the nerve to serve my specialty coffee drink on my menu. Getting out the drug game made me quite the creative with legal concoctions that pack a punch. Mixed with the creamiest of liqueurs and strong whiskey, this is about to make your mornings, or evenings, a lot more exciting. Just don't drink this within sixty feet of Grundle's or the place will be shut down.

¼ cup whiskey

1 cup nitro coffee

¼ cup Kahlúa

1 cup ice cubes

1 tablespoon caramel sauce, plus more for drizzling

Whipped cream

1. Pour the whiskey, coffee, and Kahlúa into a cocktail shaker and add the ice. Stir for 20 to 30 seconds, until completely chilled.

2. Drizzle the caramel sauce on the inside of the glass so it drips downward. Strain the cocktail into the caramel-lined glass. Top with whipped cream and drizzle on extra caramel.

BUSTA BUSTA NAC

SERVES 2

Let me tell you something I learned long ago: life will never lead you astray (or as astray as it led me) if you keep in mind the immortal words of Busta Rhymes: "Pass the Courvoisier." Much like a fat-ass blunt, passed Courvoisier is a panacea (I learned that word from Felony). Shay couldn't say nothing to me, Wavy couldn't say nothing to me, and my mama couldn't say nothing to me—so long as I had a sip of Courvoisier at hand. What I've learned since this beloved elixir came into my life is that it's even better in a mixed drink! Upgrade your life and wild-style your cocktail! Then pass me some!

1 lime

3 tablespoons cognac

1 cup ice

1 cup ginger beer

1. Slice 4 wheels from the lime.

2. In a shaker, combine the cognac, 2 of the lime wheels, and the ice. Shake vigorously for 30 seconds.

3. Strain into 2 glasses and top off each glass with ginger beer. Garnish with the remaining lime wheels.

B-BALL WATER

Shay came up with this concoction when she was trying to get Shahzad to take up basketball. Something about how it would help him look more well-rounded for college applications. But that boy doesn't have an athletic bone in his body. He still looks like a dry jellyfish on the court. But I took a liking to this drink and do believe it helps me keep my stamina going after a few rounds of dunkin' on Bobby.

FOR THE SEA MOSS GEL
1 (2 ounce) package of sea moss

FOR THE B-BALL WATER
1 tablespoon sea moss gel
1 (0.11 ounce) packet Crystal Light
2½ cups coconut water, chilled

1. **Make the Sea Moss Gel:** Wash the sea moss of any dirt or dust. Submerge the sea moss in a bowl of water and soak for at least 8 hours or overnight. Drain and wash the sea moss again under cold running water.

2. In a food processor or blender, pulse the sea moss until it is broken up into small pieces. Add ½ cup of cold water and blend until it forms a smooth gel.

3. Transfer to a jar with a lid or a plastic container. Store in the refrigerator for up to 1 week.

4. **Make the B-ball Water:** In a pitcher, whisk the sea moss gel with the Crystal Light powder and ½ cup of the coconut water to dissolve. Gradually add the rest of the coconut water. Alternatively, combine all of the ingredients in a sports bottle, cover, and shake until combined.

POUR SOME OUT

207

SHAY'S PINK DRINK

SERVES
4

Let me start by saying that I'm not one to make fancy-schmancy cocktails that need umbrellas in them. But, ever since I saw my Shay drinking this pink drink at her fundraiser, I got super into them. I thought if I perfected this drink, she'd dump Josh and take me back. Shockingly, that didn't happen. What did happen is that I got the halfway house guys so hooked on this sweet and minty drink that I fear if I stop making it, I'll face my death. As relaxing as it is delicious, this is the perfect drink to kick back with on your hand-me-down couch.

FOR THE SIMPLE SYRUP
1 cup granulated sugar
1 cup water

FOR THE PINK DRINK
1 pound strawberries, hulled
2 tablespoons simple syrup
Ice
3 cans plain seltzer
4 sprigs fresh mint leaves

1. Make the Simple Syrup: Mix the sugar and water in a small saucepan and bring to a simmer. Remove from the heat and stir to dissolve the sugar. Let the syrup cool completely. Transfer to a bottle or jar with a lid.

2. Make the Pink Drink: In a blender, blend the strawberries with the simple syrup to a smooth puree.

3. Fill each of 4 glasses with ½ cup of the strawberry puree and top them off with ice. Fill the glasses with seltzer and stir lightly with a spoon. Garnish each glass with a sprig of mint.

DOWN AT THE RINK

THE BEST PLACE TO FLEX, always and forever, will be your local roller rink. Whether it's your play sister's birthday party, a church event, or a lucky Saturday afternoon, lacing up your skates (or rollerblades if your parents had the money) meant that it was time to get all the way down. Add on a mystery meat hotdog, a large soda, and a fresh DJ— you couldn't tell us nothing rolling around that rink like it was the club. They even say that roller disco got its start in Brooklyn, at a rink near Ebbets Field on Empire Boulevard. Rinks are harder to find nowadays, but they're worth seeking out. Here are some pointers for first-timers.

FRESH FOOTWEAR

You may think you can just rent a pair of those paper-bag-colored skates and be ready, but if you want to be a real rink bitch, you better have a custom set of skates. I'm talking Adidas shoes with some wheels attached.

MAKE MOVES

Come prepared with a routine for at least a few songs. Skating in circles won't get you a man, woman, or any street cred. Link arms with some friends and channel your inner Salt-n-Pepa.

SOCK IT TO 'EM

Your socks are just as important as your skates—both in terms of style and performance. Long, thick, breathable socks are best, to keep your feet and ankles warmed-up and limber for all those dips and spins.

VANILLA SHANK

SERVES 2

4 large scoops vanilla ice cream

1 cup of ice

¼ cup whole milk

3 tablespoons Hennessy

Whipped cream

1 small square of dark chocolate

When Green Eyes joined the workforce on my food truck, he suggested this addition to our drinks menu. Just like an Aryan murderer in Rikers, this shake spiked with Hennessy will sneak up on you and kill ya! Even after just one, you may do something to get a parole violation, but it's worth it! Just like every kid wishes they could have a shake for dinner, every adult wishes they could have a shake with liquor for dinner. Even better if it's in one glass! And, because I believe that all purely vanilla things should be banned, I added a little piece of dark chocolate in there.

1. In a blender, blend the ice cream, ice, milk, and Hennessy until smooth.

2. Divide between two glasses and top each shake with whipped cream.

3. Shave the dark chocolate over the shakes and serve.

POUR SOME OUT

213

TRICK OUT A FOOD TRUCK

Every good food truck needs its own personality if you wanna stand out from the competition. Here's a blueprint of The Last Meal on Wheels's special features.

GRAFFITI SIGN

Does it still count as graffiti if you tagged your own truck on purpose and it's like a big advertisement for your business? It's still badass, though, right?

PRISON BARS

Serves two purposes: Keeping out the likes of BAMF and any other dude comes round to "collect taxes," then making the new-school Brooklynites feel like they're edgier than they actually are. Plus, the opening in the middle frames Tray's face perfectly.

ORANGE JUMPSUIT

Tray said he'd never wear one of these again, but it was either this or an apron. And the jumpsuit won.

BARBED WIRE

Don't even try climbing to the top of this truck because you'll get shredded by this truly authentic barbed wire. Somehow Green Eyes saved a couple bundles from his stints in the joint.

LOUDSPEAKER

Like the ones in each cellblock, but instead of blaring "Lockdown!" this tells you when your food is ready for pickup.

MENU BOARD

This is set up like those height charts in jail—you know, the kind you have to stand against when they're taking your mug shot. The drinks list starts at 5'9" and the entrees at 6'6".

While *The Last O.G.* may make you laugh, it also touches on some hard-hitting issues. For Tracy Morgan and all the cast and crew, one goal is to get people thinking and talking about pressing problems like criminal justice reform, mass incarceration, the challenges of re-entry for returning citizens, and food justice for minority groups. What would be even better is if the show might spur folks to get involved with organizations that are working towards solutions. From across the country, here is a selection of the many nonprofits helping in these fields.

A NEW WAY OF LIFE REENTRY PROJECT

Based in South Los Angeles and Long Beach, A New Way of Life Reentry Project is a nonprofit organization with a core mission to provide housing, case management, pro bono legal services, advocacy, and leadership development for women rebuilding their lives after prison.

anewwayoflife.org
Los Angeles, CA

BROWNSVILLE COMMUNITY CULINARY CENTER

The Brownsville Community Culinary Center is dedicated to offering healthy, accessible cuisine to its neighborhood. BCCC offers a culinary training program that educates and inspires participants to excel in the food-service industry. It offers services that support program participants as they cultivate and work toward their dreams.

meltingpotfoundationusa.org
Brooklyn, NY

DC CENTRAL KITCHEN

The goal of DC Central Kitchen's Culinary Job Training program is to prepare adults facing high barriers to employment for careers in the food service industry. The program specializes in equipping adults with histories of incarceration, addiction, homelessness, and trauma with the hands-on training and support they need to begin a culinary career.

dccentralkitchen.org
Washington, D.C.

THE DOE FUND

The Doe Fund offers a variety of holistic programs devoted to meeting the needs of a diverse population working to break the cycles of homelessness, addiction, and criminal recidivism. The Doe Fund serves thousands each day, helping homeless and formerly incarcerated individuals achieve permanent self-sufficiency.

doe.org
New York, NY

THE DREAM CORPS

The Dream Corps slogan is "21st-century jobs, not jails." It supports economic, environmental, and criminal justice innovators by connecting aspiring leaders with partners, digital resources, and media platforms. With its shared platform, The Dream Corps is reshaping the possibilities in the field of social justice.

thedreamcorps.org
Oakland, CA

DV8 KITCHEN

DV8 Kitchen offers a second-chance employment opportunity for people who are trying to redirect their lives, including those who have been formerly

Giving back to the community has been a priority for the cast and crew of *The Last O.G.* from the start. In 2017, Tracy Morgan and Cedric the Entertainer co-hosted a comedy night to raise money for the Fortune Society. In 2018, Morgan and folks from the show rallied to refurbish two public basketball courts in Brooklyn, including the one at the Marcy Playground (pictured), near the projects where Morgan grew up.

incarcerated. One out of three employees at DV8 Kitchen will be a second-chance employee. The goal is to help participants deviate from their past lifestyles and prepare for a lifetime of gainful employment. DV8 Kitchen operates a fast-casual restaurant and bakery open to the public.

dv8kitchen.com
Lexington, KY

EDWINS

EDWINS Leadership & Restaurant Institute gives formerly incarcerated adults a foundation in the culinary industry while providing a support network necessary for long-term success. Its mission is three-fold: to teach a skilled and in-demand trade in the culinary arts, empower willing minds through passion for hospitality management, and prepare students for a successful transition home. EDWINS restaurant is open for dinner six days a week.

edwinsrestaurant.org
Cleveland, OH

FARM SCHOOL NYC

Farm School NYC equips a diverse student body with the proper tools to become effective and empowered grassroots leaders in the food justice movement. They teach urban growing and planning practices as well as engage in dialogues about larger socioeconomic and justice issues in the food system. One of its partners is The Youth Farm, an education-focused production farm in Brooklyn that provides youth and adults with hands-on farm training and leadership opportunities.

farmschoolnyc.org
theyouthfarm.org
New York, NY

THE FORTUNE SOCIETY

The Fortune Society's mission is to strengthen our communities by supporting successful reentry from and promoting alternatives to incarceration. It functions on a holistic model that focuses on services in housing, employment, education, family, mental health, substance use treatment, health, food and nutrition, creative arts, and preparation for release. Their Food and Nutrition and Culinary Arts training

programs address food insecurity as one of the primary issues for incarcerated and at-risk individuals.

fortunesociety.org
Long Island City, NY

GETTING OUT AND STAYING OUT

Getting Out and Staying Out (GOSO) is one of the most successful reentry programs for justice-involved young men in the New York City area. Their aim is to promote personal, professional, and intellectual growth through early intervention within the criminal justice system as well as counseling, educational support, and workforce development.

gosonyc.org
New York, NY

GREYSTON BAKERY

Greyston's mission is to create thriving communities through the practice and promotion of Open Hiring™. With Open Hiring, Greyston is dedicated to hiring applicants without judging or asking any questions, in turn helping employees find ways to remove any obstacles to job success.

greyston.org
Yonkers, NY

HOMEBOY INDUSTRIES

Homeboy Industries provides training and support to formerly gang-involved and incarcerated men and women, offering a wide range of services to assist them in redirecting their lives. Homeboy welcomes former gang members into supportive programs including workforce development, substance abuse support, mental health, legal services, and case management in an effort to make positive change and help these individuals become contributing members of their communities.

homeboyindustries.org
Los Angeles, CA

KITCHENS FOR GOOD

Kitchens for Good aims to break the cycles of food waste, poverty, and hunger through innovative programs in workforce training, healthy food production, and social enterprise. One such program is Project Launch, a culinary apprenticeship program that trains individuals who are experiencing high unemployment rates—including foster youth transitioning out of the system, individuals with histories of substance abuse, and formerly incarcerated adults.

kitchensforgood.org
San Diego, CA

PRISON ENTREPRENEURSHIP PROGRAM

Established in 2004, the Prison Entrepreneurship Program (PEP) is committed to improving prison reentry outcomes. It offers innovative programs that equip convicted felons with the resources they need to pursue healthy, productive, and fulfilling lives once they are back in society.

pep.org
Houston, TX · Richardson, TX

REHABILITATION ENABLES DREAMS

Rehabilitation Enables Dreams (RED) is a nonprofit and restorative justice organization dedicated to keeping individuals out of the criminal justice system through a comprehensive curriculum targeting the social, financial, and civic literacy of nonviolent youths referred to court. RED's twelve-month program guides students through personal development and towards employment training to foster successful reentry into the community and decrease their chances of recidivism.

stoprecidivism.org
Atlanta, GA

SAFER FOUNDATION

Safer Foundation is one of the nation's largest nonprofit social impact organizations focusing on achieving equal employment opportunities for people with criminal records. Safer Foundation provides organizations across the country with training and technical assistance in a variety of services including education, community-based services, and workforce development.

saferfoundation.org
Chicago, IL

SECOND CHANCE

Second Chance aims to disrupt cycles of poverty and incarceration by providing workforce readiness training and opportunities for job placement and transitional housing for men and women ages eighteen and up. Its mission is to help these individuals acquire the skills, attitudes, education, and training needed to obtain sustainable employment and become self-sufficient, valuable contributors to their families, employers, and communities.

secondchanceprogram.org
San Diego, CA

THE SENTENCING PROJECT

The Sentencing Project works for a fair U.S. criminal justice system by promoting reforms in sentencing policy, addressing unjust racial disparities, and advocating for alternatives to incarceration. Its work includes media campaigns, research publications, and strategic advocacy for policy reforms.

sentencingproject.org
Washington, D.C.

SÉRÉNITÉ RESTAURANT & CULINARY INSTITUTE

Sérénité aims to change the face of recovery through food and hospitality. The restaurant has a unique mission: To eat well and do good. The goal is to instill leadership skills in men and women recovering from drug and alcohol addiction through an education in the culinary arts.

sereniterestaurant.com
Medina, OH

VERA INSTITUTE OF JUSTICE

Vera's mission is to build and improve justice systems that ensure fairness, promote safety, and strengthen communities. It works in partnership with local, state, and national government officials to tackle injustices including the causes and consequences of mass incarceration, racial disparities in the justice system, and the loss of public trust in law enforcement. Vera's projects are active in more than forty states.

vera.org
New York, NY

(Page references in *italics* refer to illustrations.)

LAST MEAL *Menu*

AMUSE-BOUCHE
Lemon Pepper Drums *(page 42)*

APPETIZER
Last Meal Pizza *(page 48)*

Busta Busta Nac *(page 205)*

MAIN COURSE
To Die Dreamin Chicken and Waffles *(page 98)*

Rose's Collard Greens *(page 138)*

Shay's Sweet Potatoes *(page 131)*

Red Kool-Aid *(page 198)*

INTERMEZZO
Pineapple Ice *(page 197)*

DESSERT
Heaven Bound Coconut Cake *(page 169)*

Image Credits

All images courtesy of Turner Entertainment Networks, Inc., except the following:

Noah Fecks: 5, 6, 12, 16, 19, 21, 24, 25, 26–27, 33, 40, 50–51, 53, 57, 62–63, 64, 69, 71, 72, 79, 83, 88, 96, 98–99, 101, 102, 107, 111 (top), 115, 116, 126, 129, 130, 149, 152–153, 160, 165, 168, 170–171, 175, 178, 183, 186, 191, 195, 196, 198–199, 201, 205, 209, 212.

Cara Howe for TBS: 105, 110 (bottom), 141.

CreativeMarket.com: 58–59, 174, 202–203

Francesco Sapienza: 10–11, 23, 36–37 (except for 3 largest images), 46–47, 48, 49 (top and bottom), 73, 89, 103, 104, 112–113, 114 (bottom), 117, 118–119, 122, 144, 146–147, 154, 156-157, 162, 163, 188–189, 194. www.francescosapienza.com

Shutterstock: Cover: RTimages (toque), AVN Photo Lab (brick wall); 4: Mandritoiu; 17, 30-31, 34 (top center), 94, 95, 204: Anna Zabella; 45: Lagui; 44-45: Russel Watkins, Stephen Rees, Picsfive; 41: Beth Van Trees; 39: Brooke Becker; 35: Valeriy Lebedev; 34 (from left): sakchaistockphoto, Sergiy Kuzmin (also on p. 128 center), Binh Thanh Bui; 49: DW labs Incorporated; 65: Niki Nykarti; 76, 79: Suwatsilp Sooksang; 78: Caftor; 82: karnaval2018; 90: guteksk7; 108 (background): Jose Gil; 108 (center): Nikolay Antonov; 108: (top): Roman Belogorodov; 123: Photo Boutique; 128 (top right): Miguel Garcia Saavedra (bottom right): Sergiy Kuzmin; 132: John Johnson; 133: Bermix Studio; 162, 163, 172, 180, 184: Picsfive

Istock: 34 (top left): joakimbkk; 128 (far left): Wragg

THIS BOOK WAS PRODUCED BY

MELCHER MEDIA
124 West 13th Street
New York, NY 10011
melcher.com

Founder, CEO: Charles Melcher
VP, COO: Bonnie Eldon
Executive Editor/Producer: Lauren Nathan
Senior Editor: Christopher Steighner
Production Director: Susan Lynch
Associate Editor/Producer: Victoria Spencer
Editor: Megan Worman
Assistant Designer/Editor: Renée Bollier
Editorial Assistant: Sharon Ettinger

Food styling by Victoria Granof
Prop styling by Christopher Spaulding

Melcher Media gratefully acknowledges the following for their contributions: Olivia Bartz, Dale View Biscuits and Beer, Tai Blanche, Deborah Brody, Shannon Fanuko, Laura Forti, Cara Howe, Karolina Manko, Anya Markowitz, Emma McIntosh, Avery Quigley, Lisa Silfen, Mariah Smith, Nadia Tahoun, MarC Theobald, and Katy Yudin.

JAYBIRD

Once guzzled three Garvey Palmers (page 193) to stay alert for his probation hearing

FELONY

Loves French Connection Fries (page 134) but picks out the mushrooms because he believes they cause toe fungus

MULLINS

Takes a daily shot of B-Ball Water (page 207) to keep up his "stamina"